THE CUISINART® FOOD PROCESSOR

PÂTÉ COOKBOOK

THE CUISINART® FOOD PROCESSOR

PÂTÉ COOKBOOK

Carmel Berman Reingold

A GD/Perigee Book

Perigee Books
are published by
The Putnam Publishing Group
200 Madison Avenue
New York, New York 10016

Cuisinart® and Cuisinarts® are registered trademarks
of Cuisinarts, Inc., 411 West Putnam Avenue,
Greenwich, CT 06830.

Library of Congress Cataloging in Publication Data

Reingold, Carmel Berman.

The Cuisinart food processor pâté cookbook
"A GD/Perigee book."
1. Pâtés (Cookery)   2. Terrines.   I. Title.
TX749.R524   1983   641.8'12   83-8122

ISBN 0-399-50856-2 (pbk.)

First Perigee printing, 1983
Printed in the United States of America
1 2 3 4 5 6 7 8 9

Thanks To . . .

The many restaurateurs and professional chefs, both in the United States and abroad, who invited me into their kitchens, and who shared their recipes and expertise with me. . . . Batia and Arthur Feldman, and Raymonde and Theo Siecat, who are *tout Paris* to me, and who traveled with me around France, helping to gather material. They also generously entertained at their own tables, serving interesting pâtés, elegant coulibiacs, and the quintessential foie gras. . . . Chantal Eisinger, who patiently and charmingly helped translate French material into proper English. . . . Harry Reingold, who happily ate pâtés with his breakfast toast, weekend lunches, and before-dinner French 75's. The ultimate *bec fin,* Harry says he never met a pâté that he didn't like. . . . Joan and Dick Schaeffer, who taste-tested with me around the Hawaiian Islands . . . Dori Lundy-Kuber, who made California infinitely hospitable . . . and Oswaldo Llorens of the Beverly Hills outpost of Trader Vic's, who re-created the tofu pâtés served to Queen Elizabeth and served them very specially to me.

Contents

CHAPTER ONE

PÂTÉS: SOME HISTORY AND A FEW DEFINITIONS

Ten years ago the popular dish making its ubiquitous rounds at dinner parties and restaurant tables was any roast meat baked in a crust—Beef Wellington was the perfect example. The en croûte (in a crust) fancy was eclipsed by the quiche fad—Lorraine, ham, spinach, scallop. Quiche has become a staple on every menu. Today pâté has become the rage, and because of the endless variety and the creative possibilities offered in pâté cookery, pâtés will be popular for years to come.

Pâté was a slow starter in the United States. Most restaurants either offered a smooth, unctuous liver blend—usually called pâté maison—or a coarse meat mixture known as pâté de campagne. Wonderful dishes, such as a salmon pâté or a terrine of sole, it seemed, could only be enjoyed at the most expensive places—certainly never at home. Any home chef checking a pâté recipe would flinch at directions that called for use of a meat grinder *and* a food mill *and* a blender; it was all too much work and trouble.

But then along came the food processor—particularly the Cuisinart® food processor—and it became clear that if you could make a meat loaf you could make a pâté, because this wonderful machine would grind the meat, chop the onions, puree the vegetables, and finely grind the fish. The world of pâtés finally was opened up to the home cook. Even professional chefs, armed with the food processor, became more adventurous and creative with pâtés.

Today, you can easily make pâtés based on classic recipes, on Nouvelle Cuisine, and on the American New Cuisine. You can experiment and create your own version of a pâté de campagne. Now, thanks to the food processor, when you offer a guest a pâté maison, the maison you're talking about is your very own. Do you prefer lighter pâtés? The colorful Egg and Vegetable Terrine may look hard, but the food processor makes it easy.

When Is It a Pâté and When Is It Terrine?

The vocabulary of the pâté is mostly French, and through the years—centuries, actually—definitions have changed slightly. Pâtés, terrines, galantines—these, and others—are all versions of the multifaceted pâté. The following definitions explain the similarities and the differences.

Pâté. Originally—and this means a few hundred years ago—in France the word pâté was used to describe a meat or fish dish completely encased in pastry and baked in an oven. A deep-dish pie is a good description of some of the first pâtés.

However, as pâtés became more popular and more varied, the definition of a pâté stretched to include other forcemeat dishes that were baked in earthenware dishes, or terrines, often without a pastry crust. Today, terrine and pâté are often used interchangeably.

Terrine. To the purist of the past, a pâté baked in a terrine, or earthenware dish. Today any pâté may be called a terrine. Most terrines are baked in dishes that are lined with strips of pork fat or bacon, and they may have a bottom crust of pastry.

The *Larousse Gastronomique,* that encyclopedia of food and wine which Escoffier described as "a model of exactitude and precision," decreed that a terrine must always be served cold, while a pâté could be served hot or cold. This little nicety is not religiously observed today.

Tourte. A hot pâté baked in a crust. It is round and pie-shaped and is usually served as a main course.

According to Carème, the great French chef born in the eighteenth century, the tourte fell out of fashion when the French merchant class decided that the tourte was too common; they preferred their pâté en croûte—a hot pâté baked in a crust, but not shaped as a pie.

Carème, who was called "The cook of kings and the king of cooks," decried such pretension, and said, "How times have changed. Our great cooks in the old days used to serve tourte at the tables of princes."

Carème, who was chef to Czar Alexander and Baron de Rothschild, continued making tourtes, remembering that he had started his career at the age of seventeen working as a tourtier for Bailly, the famous pâtissier of Paris.

Carème would be pleased—possibly amused—to learn that today a tourte is the new, chic way of presenting a pâté.

Torta. The Italian version of the French tourte. It combines Italian or Italian-style ingredients baked in a crust and served as a main course.

Pains and Gâteaux. Pains (breads) and gâteaux (cakes) were the words used many years ago in French cuisine to describe the more simple pâtés and terrines. The terms went out of fashion for a number of years, but they are now back and growing ever more popular and familiar. A pain de viandes—a meat bread—is generally a pâté formed into an oblong shape, while a gâteau de viandes—a meat cake—is usually round.

A perfectly correct translation for a pain de viandes is meat loaf, which brings us back to the idea that if you can prepare a meat loaf you can make a pâté.

Pâté Pantin. A pork, sausage, or mushroom-rice pâté baked in an oval or rectangular pastry crust. The crust is not molded in a pan; the pâté is free-form, and cooked on a baking sheet.

Galantine. The most elegant member of the pâté family, this dish is boned poultry stuffed with forcemeat, pressed back into a birdlike shape, cooked, and then usually decorated with an aspic. The galantine takes more concentration—and more time to prepare—than most pâtés.

Forcemeat. The mixture of ingredients that have been ground and combined to make the pâté. Meat stuffing, or a combination of meats, are synonyms for forcemeat.

Coulibiac. The coulibiac is an elaborate pâté, usually made with salmon, baked in a brioche crust, and served at elegant restaurants in the United States and in France. The coulibiac is not originally French, however, and the recipes for coulibiac are based on the hot fish pies of czarist Russia. A coulibiac can also be prepared with a combination of fish, or with poultry.

Rillettes. Traditionally a pâté of pork and pork fat, both of which have been cooked until they fall apart. The meat and fat are then shredded, beaten until thoroughly blended, and spooned into small crocks.

The French loved their rillettes so much that they went on to prepare them with chicken and fish as well as pork.

CHAPTER TWO

EQUIPMENT AND BASIC INFORMATION

Equipment

The Food Processor. The food processor is basic to the preparation of most of the following pâté recipes. The food processor grinds the meat and the fish, chops the vegetables, and purees the liver and other forcemeats. It also makes batches of pastry for the pâtés en croûte in a matter of minutes. In Great-Grandmother's time you'd be considered a good home chef if you "had a light hand with the pastry." Today, thanks to the food processor, everyone can have a light hand with the pastry—and in just a matter of minutes, too.

Bain-marie. Many pâtés are cooked in the oven in a bain-marie, or water-bath. There's nothing really complicated here; this device is akin to a double boiler. Simply take any pan (the bottom of an old roasting pan will do) that is large enough to hold the pâté mold, terrine, or loaf pan in which you've made the pâté. Place the bain-marie in the oven, add water and heat to boiling. Place the pâté mold, terrine, or pan in the bain-marie—the boiling water should come halfway up the side of the mold—and your pâté will cook gently and evenly.

Skewer. A long, thin skewer is used to test some pâtés to see if they're done. When inserted in the center of a fish pâté, for example, the skewer should come out dry.

Pastry Board, Rolling Pin, Pastry Cloth. If you're planning to make pâtés in a pastry crust you will need a pastry board and a rolling pin to roll out the pastry. A pastry cloth is handy when you're transferring a free-form pâté, such as a coulibiac, into a baking pan.

Baking Pan or Baking Tin. Shallow baking pans or baking tins are used for baking free-form pâtés, or any pâtés not placed in a mold.

Funnel or Bulb Baster. As a pâté en croûte or a tourte cools, the meat will shrink away from the crust. At this time wine, or a cream mixture, or an aspic can be added to the pâté, using a funnel or bulb baster.

Pâté Molds. Pâtés can be baked in a large variety of molds and dishes: hinged molds, decorated pâté molds, deep-dish pie pans, tourtières (the French version of deep-dish pie pans), terrines, ovenproof casseroles.

The decision is yours, and you may decide to immediately invest in hinged molds, which are used for many classic French pâtés en croûte. The hinged mold works much like a spring-form pan. After the pâté is baked and cooled, the sides of the mold are removed. The baked pastry is beautifully formed, and decorated with the design of the mold, which is now imprinted upon the pastry.

Decorated pâté molds are also lovely, and pâtés are served directly from such oven-proof molds, many of which have covers with carved duck or rabbit heads on top.

The Pâté Molds Hiding in Your Kitchen

Before you purchase hinged molds and decorated pâté molds, you might want to look around your kitchen at the dishes and pans you already own that will make perfect receptacles for pâtés: loaf pans, oven-proof casseroles, pie pans, soufflé dishes, crocks, in various sizes, can all be utilized for pâtés.

Loaf Pans. The standard 8-cup, 2-quart loaf pan, 9×5×3 inches is just right for most pâté recipes. Loaf pans are also available in 4-, 6-, 10- and 12-cup sizes, and if you're not sure about the size of the loaf pans you now own, you can measure them by filling each pan with water. Two pounds of raw meat is the equivalent of 4 cups, or 1 quart.

Oven-proof Casseroles. If your casserole has straight sides and is made of earthenware, you own a terrine. Casseroles come in a variety of sizes, and can be measured for volume just as you'd measure a loaf pan, by filling them with water. An attractive oven-proof casserole is fine for pâtés that you plan to serve right from the dish. A terrine or casserole does not have to be the exact size of a pâté mixture. An 8-cup terrine can hold a 6- or 7-cup pâté, and a 4-cup terrine can hold a 5-cup pâté, if the pâté is meant to be high and rounded.

Round and oval casseroles and terrines serve very well for tourtes—those two-crust pâtés that resemble deep-dish pies.

Pie Pans. Regular 8- to 10-inch pie pans can be used for gâteau de viandes as well as for smaller tourtes, while deep-dish pie pans can be used for the larger tourtes. If the recipe calls for a cover, use foil, sealing tightly around the edge of the pan.

Soufflé Dishes. Oven-proof soufflé dishes, which come in a variety of sizes, can be used for any pâté or terrine that will be served right from the dish. If a cover is needed, use foil.

Crocks. Rillettes and smooth pâtés that are meant to be spread are usually stored in, and served directly from, crocks. When preparing rillettes, it is best to use two—or more—1-cup crocks rather than one large crock. It's more attractive, traditional, and the remaining crock or crocks of rillettes will keep in the refrigerator for two to three weeks if you pour melted fat over the rillettes and let it harden as a seal.

You may have crocks in your kitchen cabinet that once housed mustard, French pâté, or jam. This is what you've been saving those too-pretty-to-throw-out-but-what-am-I-going-to-do-with-them crocks.

French jam jars, currently being sold in boxes of six, also make attractive crocks for rillettes and spreadable pâtés. Because these pâtés are served directly from their container, it's best not to use a regular canning jar or any old jam jar that will not look attractive on your table.

Single-serving soufflé dishes and custard cups also work well for a small offering of a smooth liver or vegetable pâté.

Weights. Some pâtés are weighted down after they have been cooked. This squeezes out the rendered fat, rids the pâté of any air bubbles, and makes the pâté easier to slice.

To weight a pâté, take a smaller pan than the one that holds the pâté, fit it in on top of the pâté, and then put a heavy object in the top pan. You can use canned foods, a brick, or part of a meat grinder.

Basic Information

The Use of Pork Fat. Reading the classic pâté recipes, you will probably ask, "Is all that fat necessary?" The answer is yes. If you want to make a classic pâté and have it taste like a classic pâté, don't decide to cut down or eliminate much of the fat.

The fat adds a tender, moist and smooth quality to the pâté, and some of the fat does render out during cooking. Fatback, cut into thin sheets, is the pork fat traditionally used to line the dishes in which a pâté is baked. If you find it difficult to buy fatback, you can use bacon or salt pork, if you first blanch it for 10 minutes in boiling water.

Testing the Uncooked Pâté Mixture. If you want to test a meat mixture for seasoning before you form your pâté, sauté a spoonful of the mixture in a small skillet. Cook until done, taste, and correct seasoning. Never taste the meat mixture raw.

Is the Pâté Cooked? How to determine whether a pâté is cooked thoroughly depends on the type of pâté that you're preparing. A fish pâté can be tested by piercing it with a long, thin skewer. If the pâté is cooked, the skewer will come out dry.

You can tell if a meat pâté is cooked by its physical appearance. The finished pâté should shrink away from the sides of the baking dish, and juices should be yellow without any touch of pink.

A pâté covered with crust should have yellow juices bubbling from the center vent hole in the pastry, and the pastry should be golden brown. If the pastry seems to be browning too quickly, cover with foil, but make sure to leave a vent hole open, otherwise the pastry will crack.

Unmolding a Pâté. If you want to serve a cold pâté unmolded, rather than directly from the dish in which it's been cooked, refrigerate overnight. The next day, run a knife around the inside of the baking dish and place the dish in a shallow pan of hot water for 30 to 60 seconds. Turn the pâté upside down on a serving platter. Wipe away the juices with a paper towel. Leave the fat covering undisturbed. Cut the first slice before serving, so that the pâté filling can be seen.

Keeping a Pâté. A sturdy meat pâté, such as a pâté de campagne, will taste better two days after you've made it; the flavors will have a chance to meld. A meat pâté will keep approximately one week, well refrigerated, but its texture will change rather drastically if you try to freeze it. If you have a really top-notch freezer, however, you can freeze a pâté de campagne after the meat mixture has been enclosed in the pork fat but *before* it is baked.

CHAPTER THREE

PASTRY FOR PÂTÉS

Once you've mastered the simpler pâtés in this book and you've decided to go on to something really dramatic, a pâté baked in a crust provides a stunning feast. You may be using a hinged pâté mold, or a loaf pan, or perhaps a terrine for your pâté. Or perhaps you prefer a free-form pâté, where after the filling is prepared and wrapped in its pastry case, the pâté is then baked on a baking sheet. Whichever method or equipment you use, you will need pastry—pastry that will not disappoint in flavor, or have the wrong texture for your pâté.

The perfect pastry answer for most pâtés is the French version of pie dough: pâte brisée. There are a number of recipes for pâte brisée, some with and without whole eggs, or egg yolks, some with and without sugar, and all with different types or combinations of shortening.

The two recipes that follow have worked best for the pâtés in this book. Pâte Brisée I is recommended for a light pâté, terrine, or tourte. Pâte Brisée II, which is made with eggs, is recommended for pâtés that are completely wrapped in crust, and which may be free-form, such as a pâté pantin. Pâte Brisée II is also excellent for a hearty terrine, tourte, or meat pie.

The pâte brisée recipes are interchangeable, and if you wish, you can certainly use Pâte Brisée I in place of Pâte Brisée II, simply by doubling the recipe.

Pâté Pastry and the Food Processor

The food processor has taken the mystery and the worry out of preparing pastry dough. In 60 seconds you can have a perfect batch of pâte brisée—and that's every time. If you have a small food processor and you wish to make pastry for a large pâté, make it in two batches. That will take you 2 minutes instead of 1—very little time when compared to making pastry dough by hand.

If you're worried about quantity, more is definitely better than less. When wrapping a pâté entirely in pastry, you will need enough dough to close the seams. If you have leftover pâte brisée, wrap it in foil and place it in the freezer. It will be waiting for you when you're ready to make your next pâté.

If, however, you discover halfway through the preparation of a pâté that you don't have enough pastry dough, just mix up another batch. As we said before, the food processor will do it in 60 seconds.

Prebaking Pastry Shells

To partially prebake or not to partially prebake a tourte shell or the bottom crust of a pie is the subject of some discussion, even among professional chefs. Some insist that all tourte shells must be partially baked, or the bottom crust will become soggy, while others say that the bottom crusts of their pies, tourtes, etc., never become soggy, and that they never do any partial prebaking. Some of the pâté recipes in this book call for a partially prebaked shell, while others don't. If you choose to partially prebake the bottom crust of the pâté you're preparing, follow these six easy steps:

1. Line the dish with pastry, and prick the pastry.
2. Line the pastry with aluminum foil.
3. Fill the pastry with aluminum bits that can be bought in any store that specializes in cooking equipment, or with dried beans that you can keep just for this purpose.

4. Place the shell in a preheated 450° oven and bake for 8 minutes.
5. Remove shell from oven, and remove foil with aluminum bits or beans from shell.
6. Allow shell to cool, and continue with recipe.

Brioche Pastry Dough

A few pâté recipes call for brioche pastry rather than pâte brisée. Once again the food processor provides the answer, with an easy method for preparing brioche pastry dough.

If you're planning to serve one of the coulibiacs or the Roman Torta, both of which require brioche pastry, you will have to prepare the brioche dough a day ahead of time, because it does require a night's rest in your refrigerator. Unlike pâte brisée, brioche dough does not do well in the freezer.

When to Serve a Pâté en Croûte

Pâtés wrapped in pastry come in many variations. The hearty, meat-filled tourtes are best at informal suppers and are welcome at Sunday dinners. Coarse meat pâtés wrapped in pastry are a fine addition to a party buffet and travel happily to a picnic. The coulibiacs are perfect for elegant dinners and are frequently served in France at very special New Year's Eve dinners.

Once you discover how easily you can prepare pâté pastry in a food processor, you'll be preparing pâtés en croûte quite often: They delight guests, and they make both the meal and the chef look very special.

PÂTE BRISÉE I

1½ cups all-purpose flour
½ teaspoon salt, or to taste
¼ pound butter, cut into 8 pieces
3–4 tablespoons ice water

Combine all ingredients, except for ice water, in a food processor. Process until the mixture has the texture of coarse crumbs.

With the machine on, gradually add ice water until mixture forms a ball. Refrigerate for 30 minutes before using.

PÂTE BRISÉE II

3½ cups all-purpose flour
1 teaspoon salt, or to taste
¼ pound butter, cut into 8 pieces
6 tablespoons chilled lard or vegetable shortening, cut
**   into 6 pieces**
1 egg
2–4 tablespoons ice water

Combine all ingredients, except for ice water, in a food processor. Process until the mixture has the texture of coarse crumbs.

With the machine on, gradually add ice water until mixture forms a ball. Refrigerate for 30 minutes before using.

BRIOCHE PASTRY DOUGH

⅓ cup warm milk
2 quarter-ounce packages active dry yeast
¼ teaspoon sugar
4 cups all-purpose flour
¼ cup sugar
1 teaspoon salt
5 eggs
½ pound butter, cut into 16 pieces

Pour warm milk into food processor, and sprinkle yeast and ¼ teaspoon sugar over milk. Allow to stand for 5 minutes.

Add 3 cups flour, ¼ cup sugar, salt, eggs, and butter. Process until all ingredients are thoroughly blended. Add remaining cup flour, ½ cup at a time, and process, turning machine on and off, until mixture begins to form a ball.

Place dough on a lightly floured board. Knead in additional flour, if necessary, so that dough is smooth and elastic and bounces back when touched. Place dough in a buttered bowl, cover, and allow to rise in a warm, draft-free place for 2–2½ hours, or until doubled in bulk.

Punch dough down, cover tightly, and refrigerate overnight.

CHAPTER FOUR

A LOAF OF BREAD, A BOOK OF VERSE, A SLICE OF PÂTÉ— A PICNIC!

A cold pâté can make a picnic a very special occasion, indicating that there is life beyond tuna salad sandwiches and barbecued hamburgers. The pâtés that travel best to the beach or the country are the coarse pâtés de campagne, terrines, and some rillettes. These pâtés can be eaten with the fingers, placed on slices of bread, sandwich style, or used as spreads.

The Right Bread

The bread served with a picnic pâté is important. French baguettes are fine, as are Italian whole-wheat loaves. Ficelles— the really skinny French breads—should be avoided. They dry out quickly, and you could arrive at your picnic place and discover you have nothing to slice but a stick of crusty crumbs. Russian-style black bread is also the right company for a coarse pâté.

An excellent way to prepare bread for a pâté picnic is to cut a French or Italian loaf in half, lengthwise, and spread with softened butter to which you've added pressed garlic or finely chopped parsley. Wrap the bread in foil, and slice as needed for pâté sandwiches. If you're using a Russian black bread, cut into thick slices, and butter.

A Few Additions

To complement the pâté, line a basket with foil, and fill with crudités: tiny tomatoes; rings of red, green, and yellow peppers; green onions (scallions), whose tops have been cut brush-style; and celery hearts. Someone is bound to say, "I bet you've forgotten the mustard"—even though there's nary a hot dog in sight—so store a small jar of Dijon mustard in the picnic hamper. (Most of the pâté de campagne recipes are so richly flavored that mustard will hardly be necessary.) A jar of tiny gherkin pickles or French cornichon pickles will also be greeted with cries of joy. Remember, when planning a pâté picnic, to take plenty of pâté and plenty of bread. Appetites increase in the fresh air, and it always takes longer to get to a picnic destination than everyone thought it would.

For dessert, bring watermelon cut into wedges, cascades of green and black grapes, and slices of pineapple, lightly sugared.

And to Drink . . .

A simple red wine—a Beaujolais, or a Gamay from California—is fine at a picnic. Cold ale is another good choice, and though the French might shake their heads, iced tea made with lots of fresh lemon and no sugar is welcome on a hot day with a cold pâté.

An At-Home Pâté Picnic

A pâté picnic at home makes an interesting change from the usual Sunday afternoon barbecue, and it shows what you can do with ground meat when you really try. If you're giving a pâté picnic on your own patio, where you'll be using plates and forks and things, prepare a large salad to be eaten with the pâté. Put the breads on a breadboard, with crocks of flavored butter around, and offer thinly sliced rounds of dry sausage or salami as well as the pâté.

Pâté Picnic Salad. A salad to serve at a pâté picnic held on home territory should have lots going on. A delicate little salad of Bibb or Boston lettuce is not what's needed here; instead, have two or three of the coarser lettuces: romaine, escarole, chicory, or red leaf. Two different lettuces are a must, three are even better, and one won't do.

To the lettuces, which have been torn into large pieces, add thinly sliced cabbage; thinly sliced red onion; sliced radishes; cherry tomatoes, cut in half; sliced cucumber; red, green or yellow pepper rings; pitted black olives; finely chopped parsley or dill; freshly ground black pepper; salt, if you wish; and an oil and vinegar dressing made of 4 tablespoons olive oil to 1 tablespoon wine vinegar, preferably Balsamic from Italy.

For dessert. Cut watermelon and pineapple into chunks, and macerate in a large glass bowl, with sugar, white wine, and whatever fruit liqueur or eau-de-vie you happen to have in the house—framboise is nice, Grand Marnier will also do. Serve grapes on the side, because grapes, unless they're peeled, add nothing to a fresh-fruit compote.

PICNIC PÂTÉ

1½ pounds fresh pork fat or fatback
1 pound boneless veal, cubed
1 pound boneless pork shoulder, cubed
1 pound boned ham, cubed
½ pound chicken livers, cut in half
10 cloves garlic
¼ cup heavy sweet cream (whipping cream)
3 eggs
½ cup brandy
2 teaspoons salt, or to taste
2 teaspoons freshly ground white pepper
½ teaspoon allspice
½ teaspoon cinnamon
½ cup all-purpose flour

Divide pork fat into three ½-pound pieces. Slice ½ pound of pork fat into thin slices and use to line a 3-quart terrine, allowing long ends of slices to hang over the sides of the terrine. Reserve.

Combine ½ pound of pork fat with veal and pork shoulder and, using a food processor, process until finely ground. Reserve.

Combine remaining ½ pound pork fat with ham and grind coarsely. Reserve.

Using a food processor or blender, puree chicken livers with garlic, cream, eggs, and brandy.

In a large bowl, combine ground-meat mixtures with liver puree. Stir in seasonings and flour. Mix until all ingredients are thoroughly combined.

Spoon meat mixture into prepared terrine and fold overhanging strips of pork fat over top. Cover tightly with foil and place terrine in a bain-marie in a preheated 400° oven. Bake for 3 hours.

Remove terrine from oven, discard foil, and bake for an additional 20 minutes, or until top of pâté is brown.

Remove from oven and weight pâté.

Allow pâté to cool and refrigerate with weights overnight.

Serves 15 to 20.

PAIN DE VIANDE BARBECUED

3 pounds beef, cubed
Salt and freshly ground black pepper to taste
1 small onion
4 eggs
1 cup corn-bread stuffing
4 tablespoons melted butter
2 cups chicken broth
¼ cup finely chopped parsley
½ cup grated Parmesan cheese

Combine beef, salt, pepper, onion, and 3 eggs in a food processor and grind until all ingredients are thoroughly combined. Form into an oblong, 10×12 inches, on a large piece of heavy-duty foil.

Combine stuffing, butter, broth, remaining egg, and parsley in food processor. Mix thoroughly and shape stuffing mixture into a long roll running down center of the meat.

Using the foil to lift, wrap the ground-beef mixture around the stuffing mixture, completely enclosing it in the meat.

Wrap foil tightly around meat roll and twist ends to seal. Place roll on a barbecue grill 6 inches above gray coals. Cook for 1 to 1½ hours, turning roll every 10 minutes to prevent burning. Remove meat roll to a platter and discard foil. Sprinkle with Parmesan cheese.

Serves 8.

CLEMENTE AND MARISA'S ROMAN TORTA

Clemente and Marisa live in Rome, but do most of their enter-taining a few miles outside the city in their small country house. The house is located next to a railroad track used only occasion-ally by a two-car local train that goes from village to village with a great ringing of bells and tooting of whistles. When a train is about to go by, a wooden barrier drops and, because of the house's location, no one can leave until the train passes.

On most warm Sundays, Clemente and Marisa's friends feel free to arrive from Rome without prior announcement or formal invi-tation, and lunch is usually served in a grape arbor for twenty or more people who have just dropped in. The menu includes a salad of the freshest ingredients available that day, a pasta dish with chopped fresh tomatoes, fresh basil, and newly pressed olive oil, and this torta filled with Swiss chard, cheese, and thinly sliced sausage. White wine flows endlessly from demijohns that have been placed on the porch earlier in the day, and neighboring farmers and their wives come by to eat and help serve the meal. Around five o'clock, guitars appear, and there is music and sing-ing until late at night, when the hosts and the guests pile into their cars for the drive back to Rome.

2 large bunches Swiss chard
¼ teaspoon salt, optional
1 cup ricotta cheese
¼ teaspoon oregano
4 eggs
Butter
Brioche pastry dough (page 24)
¾ pound dried Italian sausage, may be a mixture of hot and mild, thinly sliced

Salt and freshly ground black pepper to taste
1 pound fresh, imported buffalo mozzarella cheese or do-
   mestic mozzarella, thinly sliced
1 egg, lightly beaten

Prepare brioche dough and reserve in refrigerator overnight.

Separate chard leaves from stalks. Wash thoroughly and place leaves in a large saucepan. Add salt, cover, and cook over medium heat until tender—about 10 to 15 minutes. Drain and squeeze out excess moisture. Place Swiss chard in a food processor and add ricotta cheese and oregano. Process until chard is finely chopped and all ingredients are thoroughly mixed. Reserve.

Prepare two 2-egg omelettes. Reserve.

Roll out three-quarters of the brioche dough and press into a buttered 9-inch flat-bottomed springform pan or deep (10-cup) layer-cake pan. Dough should come up the sides of the pan. Place half the sliced sausage on the dough. Top with one omelette, salt and pepper, half the chard-ricotta mixture, and half the sliced mozzarella.

Repeat layers: sausage, omelette, salt and pepper, chard-ricotta mixture, mozzarella.

Roll out remaining dough and fit over top of layers, sealing edges carefully inside the pan.

Brush top of dough with beaten egg and bake torta in a preheated 350° oven for 40 to 50 minutes, or until pastry is golden brown.

Cool for 15 minutes before removing from pan.

Serves 8 to 10.

PÂTÉ DE CAMPAGNE FROM LYONS

1½ pounds pork, cubed
¼ pound beef, cubed
½ pound lard
½ pound fatback
4 ounces brandy
½ cup dry white wine
2 cloves garlic, pressed
⅛ teaspoon thyme
6 crushed juniper berries
Salt and freshly ground black pepper to
  taste
4 tablespoons lard
2 large onions, chopped
1 egg, beaten
2 tablespoons all-purpose flour
Fatback to line terrine and cover pâté

Using a food processor, coarsely grind pork, beef, ½ pound lard, and ½ pound fatback. Spoon into a large bowl and add brandy, wine, garlic, thyme, juniper berries, and salt and pepper. Cover and refrigerate overnight.

Heat 4 tablespoons lard in a skillet and sauté onion until translucent. In a small bowl, combine egg and flour, mix into a paste, and add to onion in skillet. Cook, stirring, for 1 minute.

Add onion-flour mixture to ground meats and mix thoroughly.

Line a 2-quart terrine with strips of fatback. Spoon meat mixture into terrine, smooth top, and cover with slices of fatback. Cover with foil and bake in a bain-marie in a preheated 350° oven for 2 hours. Remove foil and cook pâté for an additional

30 minutes, or until top is brown and sides have pulled away from terrine.

Weight and cool. Refrigerate with weight for 8 hours.

Serves 8 to 12.

TOURTE DE VIANDES BURGUNDY

1 pound veal, cubed
1 pound boiled ham, cubed
1 pound pork, cubed
1 pound calf's liver, cubed
Salt and freshly ground pepper to taste
½ teaspoon quatre-épices (page 211)
¼ teaspoon Herbes de Provence
1 cup beef broth
½ cup red Burgundy
2 tablespoons rendered goose or chicken fat, or melted
   butter
½ pound chicken livers, cut in half
3 tablespoons butter
⅛ teaspoon nutmeg
Pâte brisée II (page 23)
½ cup red Burgundy

Using a food processor, grind veal, ham, pork, and calf's liver until coarsely ground. Place meats in a large bowl and add salt, pepper, quatre-épices, Herbes de Provence, beef broth, ½ cup wine, and melted fat or butter. Mix thoroughly and reserve.

Sauté chicken livers in 3 tablespoons butter for 3 to 4 minutes. Livers should remain pink inside. Season with nutmeg.

Line a 5-quart oven-proof casserole or terrine with pastry and spoon in half the meat mixture. Top with sautéed chicken livers and juices from pan. Cover livers with remaining meat mixture and cover meat with top crust of pastry, sealing edges carefully. Cut a small hole in the center of the pastry and prick pastry with a fork.

Bake in a preheated 400° oven for 15 minutes. Reduce heat

and bake for 1 hour. If pastry browns too quickly, cover top with foil, making sure to keep vent hole open.

After tourte is cooked, use a funnel or baster and pour remaining half cup of wine into tourte. Allow tourte to rest for 15 minutes before slicing. Serve hot or cold.
Serves 18 to 20.

RUSTIC PÂTÉ WITH BRUSSELS SPROUTS

½ pound brussels sprouts (*or* one 10-ounce package fro-
    zen brussels sprouts, thawed)
2 bay leaves
1 pound pork, cubed
1 small onion
3 slices stale or dry white bread
1 cup chicken broth
2 eggs
Salt and freshly ground black pepper to taste
Butter
Pâte Brisée II (page 23)
1 egg yolk, beaten

Cut a small, shallow cross in bottom of each brussels sprout and parboil in boiling water with bay leaves until just tender—about 10 minutes. Drain, and discard bay leaves. Reserve.

Using a food processor, grind pork with brussels sprouts and onion. Soften bread in broth and add with eggs. Mix thoroughly and season.

Butter a 2-quart terrine, pâté mold, or a 9×5×3-inch loaf pan. Roll out pâte brisée. Spoon meat mixture onto center of pastry and fold pastry over meat, tucking in ends and sealing all seams carefully. Brush with beaten egg and place seam side down in terrine. Brush top with beaten egg yolk. Cut a small hole in center of pastry and pierce pastry in two or three places with a fork.

Bake in a preheated 375° oven for 1¼ hours, or until pastry is golden brown. May be served hot or cold.

Serves 6.

TERRINE DE LAPIN AUX NOISETTES DE NEVA

1 pound chicken livers, cut in half
4 ounces port wine
1 rabbit, boned, meat finely diced (about 2 pounds of meat)
1 pound pork sausage meat
1 egg, lightly beaten
¼ teaspoon thyme
2 medium onions, finely chopped
1 cup chopped parsley
2 ounces cognac
10 hazel nuts
Salt and freshly ground black pepper to taste
Pork fatback slices to line and cover terrine
1 bay leaf

Marinate the chicken livers in the port wine for 20 minutes.

In a large bowl, combine the rabbit meat with the sausage meat, egg, thyme, onions, parsley, cognac, and hazel nuts. Mix thoroughly.

Line a 2-quart terrine with half the fatback. Spoon half the meat mixture into the terrine and smooth over. Top with chicken livers and port and cover with the remaining meat mixture. Smooth over and top with bay leaf and fatback, covering meat mixture completely.

Cover pan tightly with aluminum foil and bake terrine in a bain-marie in a preheated 350° oven for 2 hours.

Allow pâté to cool with foil cover on for 1 hour.

Serves 8 to 12.

COUNTRY-STYLE TERRINE FROM CALIFORNIA

1¼ pounds shoulder of pork, cubed
1¼ pounds beef, cubed
1¼ pounds veal, cubed
6 cloves garlic
1 small onion
2 eggs
1 cup bread crumbs
4 teaspoons salt, or to taste
2 teaspoons freshly ground black pepper
½ cup brandy
Fatback slices to line terrine
1 bay leaf

Combine pork, beef, veal, garlic, onion, eggs, bread crumbs, salt, pepper, and brandy in a food processor and grind until meats are coarsely ground and all ingredients are thoroughly combined.

Line a 3-quart terrine with fatback slices and spoon in the pâté mixture, pressing down to compact. Top with bay leaf. Place two strips of fatback crosswise on top of pâté.

Cover terrine and bake in a bain-marie in a preheated 350° oven for 1¾ hours.

Remove from oven and weight pâté. Allow pâté to cool and refrigerate with weight overnight.

Serves 15 to 20.

SPICY CHICKEN LIVER RILLETTES

1 pound chicken livers
½ pound sliced bacon, coarsely chopped
1 medium onion, chopped
4 cloves garlic, sliced
4 bay leaves
1 teaspoon salt, or to taste
¼ teaspoon hot red pepper
2 tablespoons Worcestershire sauce
½ teaspoon ground nutmeg
1 teaspoon dry mustard
⅛ teaspoon ground cloves

Place livers, bacon, onion, garlic, bay leaves, salt, red pepper, and Worcestershire sauce in a large skillet. Cover and cook over low heat for 20 minutes. Livers and bacon will release enough moisture and fat so that no extra liquid will be needed.

Remove bay leaves and allow liver mixture to cool for 10 minutes.

Using a food processor, process all ingredients from skillet with remaining seasonings until mixture is smooth and thoroughly combined.

Spoon into a crock and refrigerate for 4 to 6 hours before serving.

Serves 6 to 8.

RILLETTES OF CHICKEN FROM BRESSE

1 chicken (2½–3 pounds), cut into eighths
1 pound fatback, or salt pork, which has been blanched
   for 10 minutes
2 cups dry white wine
1 teaspoon ground thyme
1 bay leaf
Salt and freshly ground white pepper to taste
½ cup rendered goose or chicken fat

Remove skin of chicken and cut skin into large pieces.

Combine chicken, chicken skin, fatback, wine, and seasonings in a large, heavy pot. Add enough water to cover. Bring to a simmer and cook over a low heat for 3½ hours. Add rendered goose or chicken fat and cook an additional 30 minutes.

Remove from heat, and using a slotted spoon, remove pieces of chicken and place on a large board. Allow chicken to cool until it can be easily handled. Bone chicken. Discard bones and pieces of chicken skin still in pot. Reserve cooking liquid.

Shred chicken by giving it one quick whirl in a food processor. Using a whisk, beat shredded chicken, gradually adding liquid until thoroughly combined. Correct seasoning and spoon rillettes into two or three small crocks.

Serves 6 to 8.

CHAPTER FIVE

IMPRESSIVE BEGINNINGS

Appetizers, hors d'oeuvres, the first course offered to guests are for many the best part of a meal. Pâtés are a wonderful change from the ubiquitous round of Brie or the dish of salted nuts, and the pâté you serve as an appetizer or a first course depends on the occasion.

If the pâté is meant to be a prelude to a large dinner, it should be comparatively light, so that your guests can enjoy the remainder of the meal, but if you plan to serve pâtés at a cocktail party, prepare some of the richer terrines. Cocktail parties have been known to continue to—and through—the dinner hour, and if the party is a good one and no one feels like going home, your pâtés can be a fulfilling meal.

If pâtés are going to be the centerpiece of a party, be sure to offer a variety. A pâté de campagne is wonderful for this and most other occasions. Slice half the pâté as thinly as possible—not too thin, or the slices will fall apart—and have slices of pumpernickel and French bread strategically placed nearby. When served in manageable slices, pâté becomes finger food.

In addition, have a pot or two of rillettes placed around the room with French bread rounds, as well as the largest crackers you can find. Teeny, tiny crackers will not allow anyone to do justice to rillettes.

If you're planning on a pâté as a first course, serve a seafood pâté or a vegetable terrine. They're light enough not to spoil the appetite for dinner, and they're so festive that they will create that impressive beginning.

EGG AND VEGETABLE TERRINE

5 large tomatoes, peeled, seeded, coarsely chopped
2 tablespoons tomato paste
2 tablespoons cornstarch
1 cup crème fraîche (page 210)
9 eggs, beaten
Salt and freshly ground black pepper to taste
Butter
2 cups cooked chopped spinach
1 cup grated Swiss cheese
½ cup crème fraîche
8 ounces Golden Caviar
Caviar Sauce (page 199)

Place tomatoes in a saucepan and cook, stirring, over medium heat until most of the juices have evaporated. You should have approximately 1 cup of tomato pulp. Turn off heat, stir in tomato paste. Combine thoroughly and reserve.

In a small bowl, combine cornstarch and 1 cup crème fraîche and mix until thoroughly blended.

Add seasoning to beaten eggs and combine with cornstarch-crème fraîche mixture. Mix thoroughly and reserve.

Butter a 6-cup terrine or loaf pan and butter a piece of waxed paper cut to fit bottom of terrine. Line terrine with waxed paper.

Combine spinach with a third of the egg mixture. Mix thoroughly and spoon into terrine. Place terrine in a bain-marie and bake in a preheated 300° oven for 40 to 45 minutes, or until egg-spinach layer is set.

Remove terrine from oven. Combine tomatoes with half the

remaining egg mixture. Mix well and spoon over spinach layer in terrine. Return terrine to bain-marie in oven and bake for 40 to 45 minutes, or until tomato layer is set.

Remove terrine from oven and stir cheese into remaining egg mixture, mixing well. Spoon egg-cheese mixture into terrine and return terrine to bain-marie in oven and bake for 40 to 45 minutes, or until cheese layer is set.

Allow pâté to cool before refrigerating for 8 hours, or overnight.

Turn pâté out of terrine onto a platter. Remove waxed paper. Using a spatula, spread ½ cup crème fraîche over top layer of terrine, smoothing to even. Place in refrigerator for 15 minutes.

Spread Golden Caviar over crème fraîche and refrigerate pâté until ready to serve. Serve with Caviar Sauce.

Serves 8 to 10.

PÂTÉ POSTSCRIPT: GOLDEN CAVIAR

The happy news for caviar lovers is the appearance of Golden Caviar, the whitefish roe that has been allowed to remain its natural, golden-apricot color. Golden Caviar has a delicate, nonfishy flavor, may be kept in the freezer, and is a fraction of the price of imported, sturgeon caviar. Golden Caviar may be used when preparing pâtés, or in sauces to be served with pâtés.

SWEDISH PÂTÉ OF SMOKED FISH

1½ pounds of fillets of smoked trout
½ pound smoked salmon
Juice of 1 lemon
2 teaspoons Worcestershire sauce
¼ teaspoon hot pepper sauce or Tabasco
1 cup heavy sweet cream (whipping cream)
Salt to taste

Be sure that all bones are removed from trout. Cut trout into large pieces and place in a food processor.

Cut smoked salmon into large pieces and add to trout. Start processing and gradually add lemon juice, Worcestershire sauce and hot pepper sauce or Tabasco. When mixture is a smooth, thick puree, spoon into a large bowl and gradually stir in heavy sweet cream. Add salt, if you wish. Smoked fish is usually quite salty, and additional salt may not be necessary.

Spoon fish pâté into a 6-cup terrine or crock. Cover with foil and refrigerate 3 to 5 hours, or until chilled.

Serve with an assortment of crudités: leaves of endive, slices of white and black radish, cooked sliced beets, and thinly sliced rye toast.

Serves 8 to 10.

TERRINE OF SOLE AND BASS WITH WATERCRESS SAUCE

Rich in flavor and textures, this French terrine combines a delicate fish puree with fillets of bass, the entire dish served with a sauce that combines peppery watercress with unctuous crème fraîche. Elegant enough to open any dinner party, it takes a surprisingly short time to prepare.

> **1 pound fillets of sole or flounder**
> **2 egg whites**
> **2 cup crème fraîche (page 210)**
> **⅛ teaspoon ground nutmeg**
> **Salt and freshly ground white pepper to taste**
> **1 pound fillets of bass, thinly sliced**
> **Butter**
> **Watercress Sauce (page 189)**

Using a food processor, puree fillets of sole or flounder, gradually adding egg whites, crème fraîche, nutmeg, salt and pepper.

Butter a 3-quart terrine or round mold and place a layer of fillets of bass on bottom of terrine. Cover with a layer of puree of fish and continue layering, finishing with a layer of fish puree.

Place terrine in a bain-marie in a preheated 350° oven for approximately 40 minutes, or until a thin skewer inserted into center of terrine comes out clean.

Unmold terrine onto a serving platter and spoon warm Watercress Sauce over and around terrine.

Serves 8 to 10.

RILLETTES DE SAUMON

This rillettes combines both fresh and smoked salmon and is served at Restaurant Julien in Paris. It's a simple dish to prepare, and its success depends on the flavor of the fish. The fresh salmon must be really fresh and the smoked salmon should be the best you can buy. French smoked salmon is generally smokier and a little dryer than American salmon; West Coast smoked salmon comes closest to the French version in both flavor and texture.

> **4 tablespoons olive oil**
> **½ pound fillet or steak of fresh salmon**
> **Salt and freshly ground white pepper to taste**
> **2 tablespoons brandy or cognac**
> **¼ pound sweet butter**
> **½ pound smoked salmon**
> **¼ pound sweet butter, softened**

Heat oil in a skillet. Cut the fresh salmon into cubes and sauté in the skillet, stirring, just until salmon flakes. Do not let salmon pieces brown. Spoon salmon and juices from skillet into a bowl. Season, and sprinkle with brandy or cognac. Reserve.

Wash skillet, or use another skillet, and heat ¼ pound of butter. Cut smoked salmon into large pieces and sauté in skillet, stirring. Do not let smoked salmon brown. Using a slotted spoon, transfer smoked salmon pieces to food processor, and allow to cool for 15 minutes.

Add softened butter to smoked salmon and process just until salmon is shredded and thoroughly combined with butter.

Add fresh salmon to smoked salmon in food processor and

process until thoroughly combined. Correct seasoning. Spoon salmon rillettes into a 6-cup terrine and refrigerate for 8 hours.

Serve as first course, with a chilled bottle of dry white wine.

Serves 4 to 6.

RILLETTES OF CHICKEN LIVERS WITH SHRIMP SAUCE À LA BRILLAT-SAVARIN

1 or 2 medium-to-large marrow bones
¾ pound chicken livers, cut in half
4 tablespoons beef stock, or reduced beef broth
3 eggs, lightly beaten
4 tablespoons butter, softened
1 shallot
Salt and freshly ground white pepper to taste
Butter
Shrimp Sauce (page 193)

Poach marrow bones in boiling water for 15 minutes, or roast in a 350° oven for 15 minutes. Allow bones to cool until they can be easily handled and, using a small spoon or knife, scoop marrow out of bones and discard bones. You should have about ½ cup of marrow.

Using a food processor, puree and combine all ingredients except for Shrimp Sauce. Butter a 6-cup pâté mold, crock, or terrine, and spoon liver-marrow mixture into mold. Cover mold with foil.

Place pâté mold in a large pot on top of the stove. Pour enough cold water in pot to come halfway up the sides of the pâté mold. Bring water to a simmer—do not let the water boil—and cook for 1½ hours. Serve with Shrimp Sauce.

Serves 4 to 6.

WALNUT PÂTÉ EN GELÉE

½ cup toasted walnuts
1 pound chicken livers
1 small onion, chopped
2 cups chicken broth
¼ teaspoon thyme
¼ pound plus 4 tablespoons butter, softened
Salt and freshly ground black pepper to taste
1 tablespoon brandy
Butter
1 tablespoon (1 packet) unflavored gelatin
1 cup dry white wine
Sliced green olives, walnut halves, chopped pimiento,
   chopped green pepper for garnish

Coarsely chop toasted walnuts in a food processor and reserve.

Cut livers in half. In a skillet, combine livers with onion, 1 cup broth, and thyme and sauté for 10 minutes, or until livers are firm but still slightly pink inside. Allow to cool for ten minutes.

Using a food processor, puree liver mixture with pan juices, adding butter, about 2 tablespoons at a time, and processing after each addition. Add seasonings, brandy, and walnuts, and process until just combined.

Line bottoms and ends of two 5½×2¼-inch loaf pans with a strip of parchment or waxed paper. Butter paper and sides of pans. Spoon the pâté mixture into the two pans and smooth surface. Cover pans and chill 4 to 6 hours.

To unmold: loosen sides with small spatula and invert pâtés onto a flat pan. Lift off paper. Return to refrigerator.

Soften gelatin in wine. Heat remaining 1 cup broth and add to wine-gelatin mixture, stirring to dissolve. When gelatin begins to thicken and set, spoon a layer over each of the loaves. Return to refrigerator to set. Use a second portion of the gelatin to make a second layer on pâté loaves and chill again.

Make a decorative arrangement of the olive slices, walnut halves, pimiento and green pepper on top of each pâté. Spoon thickened gelatin over decorations and chill. Repeat until all gelatin is used up and again chill pâtés.

To serve, lift loaves onto serving platters. Gelatin which has dropped off may be chopped and used as garnish around loaves.

Serves 6 to 8.

CHICKEN AND GOOSE LIVER PÂTÉ WITH CELERY

3 tablespoons rendered goose fat, if available, or butter
1 cup celery, chopped coarsely
1 small onion, chopped coarsely
½ pound chicken livers, cut in half
1 large goose liver, cut into 4 pieces
¼ cup chicken broth
Salt and freshly ground black pepper to taste
2 hard-cooked eggs, sliced crosswise
Paprika to taste

Heat goose fat or butter in a large skillet. Add celery, onion, chicken livers, and goose liver to skillet and sauté, stirring, until livers are firm, but pink inside.

Using a food processor, combine contents of skillet with broth, salt and pepper and process until mixture is smooth and thoroughly blended.

Spoon mixture into a 3-cup terrine and refrigerate 6 to 8 hours. Pâté may be unmolded or served directly from the terrine. Decorate pâté with slices of egg and a dusting of paprika.

Serves 6 to 8.

PARTY-TIME OLIVE PÂTÉ

Here is a vegetable pâté that's easily prepared two at a time. The result can be a colorful addition to a large party, an important Sunday brunch, or a buffet. Should there be pâté left, it will be welcome the following day at tea or cocktail time.

½ **pound butter**
2 **cups minced onion**
2 **cloves garlic, mashed**
1 **teaspoon chopped green onion (scallion)**
4 **cups chopped pitted black olives (California ripe olives), drained**
1 **teaspoon lemon juice**
1 **cup cooked carrot puree**
1 **teaspoon fresh minced mint**
1 **cup cooked green pea puree**
3 **tablespoons gelatin (3 packets)**
1¼ **cups cold water**
¼ **teaspoon hot pepper sauce or Tabasco**
1 **cup minced parsley**
1 **cup coarsely chopped pimiento peppers**

Heat butter in a skillet. Sauté onion, garlic, and green onion for 3 minutes, stirring. Add olives and cook, stirring, until all liquid in skillet is absorbed. Reserve.

Stir lemon juice into carrot puree and reserve. Stir mint into green pea puree and reserve.

Soften gelatin in cold water and cook over low heat, stirring, until gelatin is completely dissolved. Reserve.

Using a food processor, puree olive mixture with hot pepper sauce and parsley. Add ¾ cup dissolved gelatin to olive puree and blend thoroughly. Reserve.

Blend ¼ cup gelatin with carrot puree, mixing thoroughly. Reserve. Blend ¼ cup gelatin with green pea puree, mixing thoroughly. Reserve.

Assemble loaves in two 1-quart loaf pans. Spoon 1¼ cups of olive mixture into bottom of each pan. Smooth over. Top with a ½-cup layer of green pea puree, smooth over, and follow with a ½-cup layer of carrot puree. Smooth once again and finish with remaining 1¼ cups of olive puree. Chill until firm, approximately 4 to 6 hours.

Unmold and garnish with chopped pimiento.

Serves 12 to 15.

PÂTÉ BRASSERIE-STYLE

½ pound veal, cubed
½ pound lean pork, cubed
½ pound fatback
4 tablespoons butter
1 large onion, finely chopped
2 cloves garlic, finely chopped
¼ teaspoon allspice
¼ teaspoon mace
Salt and freshly ground black pepper to taste
½ pound chicken livers, coarsely chopped
1 cup heavy sweet cream (whipping cream)
½ cup cognac
3 eggs, beaten
½ pound cooked fresh ham, cut into ½-inch strips
Butter

Using a food processor, grind veal, pork, and fatback. Spoon meat mixture into a large bowl. Reserve.

Heat 4 tablespoons butter in a skillet and sauté onion and garlic until onion is translucent. Add onion-garlic and juices from skillet to meat mixture. Add all other ingredients, except for ham, to meat mixture and stir to combine.

Butter a 3-quart terrine and spoon a third of the meat mixture into terrine. Smooth top and place half of ham strips on top. Cover with another third of the meat mixture, smooth, and top with remaining ham strips.

Spoon in remaining meat mixture and smooth again.

Cover terrine with lid or foil and bake in a bain-marie in a preheated 350° oven for 2 hours.

Remove cover and bake another 30 minutes. Weight and cool. Refrigerate for 24 hours.

Serves 10 to 15.

PÂTÉ OF VEAL MACADAMIA

1½ pounds veal, cut into cubes
1½ pounds pork, cut into cubes
¼ pound fatback, cut into small dice
½ pound mushrooms, sliced
3 shallots, finely chopped
1 tablespoon brandy
1½ pounds calf's liver, cut into 1-inch cubes
½ teaspoon thyme
½ cup heavy sweet cream (whipping cream)
¼ teaspoon mace
½ cup chopped macadamia nuts
½ pound tongue, cut into cubes
Salt and freshly ground black pepper to taste
½ pound fatback, cut into strips
1 bay leaf
Horseradish Cream Sauce (page 199)

Using a food processor, coarsely grind veal and pork. Reserve.

Sauté ¼ pound diced fatback in a large skillet. Cook until fat renders and fatback pieces start to brown. Add mushrooms and shallots to skillet and cook, stirring, for 3 minutes. Add brandy and cook another minute.

Add liver to skillet and cook, stirring, for 3 to 5 minutes. Liver should remain faintly pink inside, or it will toughen.

Using a food processor, puree fatback-liver mixture with all juices from skillet. Add this puree to veal-pork mixture and mix thoroughly.

Add all other ingredients, except for strips of fatback, bay leaf, and Horseradish Cream Sauce, to meat mixture and mix thoroughly to combine.

Line a 3-quart pâté mold with fatback strips, allowing ends of fatback to hang over sides. Spoon meat mixture into the mold and smooth the top. Place bay leaf in center of the pâté and bring over ends of fatback, so that pâté is completely covered.

Cover pâté with foil and bake in a bain-marie in a preheated 350° oven for 2 hours.

Allow pâté to cool for 1 hour. Weight pâté and refrigerate overnight. Serve with Horseradish Cream Sauce.

Serves 20 to 25.

BELGIAN TERRINE
WITH PRUNES

½ pound pitted prunes
1 cup dry white wine
3 tablespoons brandy
1 pound pork liver
1 pound pork fatback or blanched bacon
Salt and freshly ground black pepper to taste
1 large onion, thinly sliced

Marinate prunes in wine and brandy for 1 hour, turning prunes and spooning liquid over them from time to time.

Using a food processor, grind liver and fatback or bacon coarsely. Add prunes with liquid and seasonings and process until prunes are coarsely chopped and all ingredients are combined.

Spoon mixture into a 2-quart terrine. Top with onion slices and cover.

Bake in a preheated 325° oven for 1½ hours. Weight and cool. Refrigerate for 8 hours.

Serves 6 to 8.

RILLETTES DE PORC

Pork rillettes consists of shreds of meat suspended in rendered fat. The best way to arrive at the right texture is to cook the pork for many hours over low heat, then shred the meat using a food processor and a fork or whisk. Rillettes must not be overprocessed to ultimate smoothness—that's fine for a delicate liver pâté, but absolutely wrong for rillettes.

> 1 pound pork fatback or blanched bacon, cut into small
>   cubes
> 2 pounds pork shoulder, cut into small cubes
> Salt and freshly ground black pepper to taste
> 2 whole cloves garlic
> 1 small onion

Place the fatback or bacon in a large, heavy pot and cook over very low heat until some of the fat renders, approximately 15 minutes. If you think your pot is not heavy enough, place it on a Flame Tamer or the bottom part of a top-of-the-stove potato baker. The fatback must not brown or become crisp.

Add all other ingredients to pot, cover, and cook over low heat for 3 hours. Remove the onion and discard, and cook for an additional 1 to 2 hours, or until meat is falling apart. Drain off fat and reserve. Allow meat and fat to cool for 30 minutes.

Meat must now be reduced to shreds and combined with some or all of the fat. If meat is really tender, it may be possible to shred it with a fork. If not, drop meat cubes into a food processor and pulse on and off quickly—do not overprocess.

After the meat is shredded, beat in as much fat as you wish, using a fork or whisk. Mixture will whiten as you beat, but do not overbeat, because texture of the rillettes should remain coarse.

Spoon rillettes into crocks or French jelly glasses and cover. Chill thoroughly before serving with slices of French bread.

Rillettes is excellent as a first course or as a party dish. It is rich and smooth and should be followed by a light main course.

Serves 15 to 20.

RILLETTES OF OLIVES

1½ **cups drained, pitted black olives (California ripe olives)**
1 **cup grated cheddar or Swiss cheese**
2 **hard-cooked eggs**
1 **tablespoon brandy**
¾ **teaspoon dried basil**
Salt and freshly ground black pepper to taste
1 **clove garlic**
2 **green onions (scallions), minced**

Combine all ingredients, except green onion, in a food processor. Puree until almost completely smooth. Spoon into a 2-cup crock and cover. Chill for 2 to 4 hours before serving.

Sprinkle with minced green onion and serve with French bread or crackers.

Yield: 2 cups, approximately

A POPULAR PÂTÉ INGREDIENT: CHICKEN LIVERS

Chicken livers are one of the main ingredients found in many meat pâtés, and this versatile food also makes an excellent pâté by itself, when combined with a variety of spices or other seasonings.

The following recipes indicate some of the ways that chicken livers can become flavorful pâtés. Remember when sautéing livers not to cook them until they are well done. Overcooked chicken livers will have a dry and grainy texture, and they are best when cooked until firm, but slightly pink inside.

PÂTÉ OF CHICKEN LIVERS IN A CROCK

1 cup, or more, rendered chicken fat
1 pound chicken livers
1 large onion
Salt and freshly ground black pepper to taste
3 red radishes, thinly sliced

Heat chicken fat in a large skillet. Place chicken livers in skillet and sauté until they are firm, but pink inside.

Using a food processor, process livers and onion until mixture is combined into a smooth puree. Season to taste.

Spoon pâté into a 3-cup crock and decorate with radish slices. Chill 6 to 8 hours before serving.

Serve with pumpernickel or black bread.

Serves 8.

CURRIED CHICKEN LIVER PÂTÉ

¼ pound butter
½ teaspoon curry powder
½ cup chopped green onions (scallions)
2 pounds chicken livers
⅓ cup brandy
½ cup parsley
Salt and freshly ground black pepper to taste
Parsley for garnish

In a skillet, heat 4 tablespoons of butter with curry powder until bubbly; add onions and chicken livers. Cook over low heat until livers lose their pink color and are firm.

Using a food processor, process contents of skillet with remainder of butter, the brandy, and parsley, until mixture is smooth and well mixed. Add seasoning. Mix thoroughly. Spoon into a 6-cup crock.

Cover and chill several hours or overnight to mellow flavors and firm mixture. Garnish with additional parsley.

Serves 8 to 12.

BRANDIED PÂTÉ

¼ pound butter
1 pound chicken livers, cut in half
1 medium onion, grated
¼ pound mushrooms, coarsely chopped
½ cup brandy
Salt and freshly ground black pepper to taste
¼ teaspoon cumin

Heat butter in a large skillet and sauté livers until firm, but pink inside. Livers should not be overcooked or they will become too dry. Using a slotted spoon, remove livers from skillet and place in food processor.

Add onion and mushrooms to skillet and sauté, stirring, until onions are translucent and mushrooms have released their liquid.

Add contents of skillet to livers, and process until just combined. Mushroom pieces should not be pureed. Stir in brandy and seasonings, mix well, and spoon pâté into a 3-cup crock. Chill for 4 to 6 hours.

Serves 6 to 8.

OYSTER-ALMOND PÂTÉ

Two 8-ounce packages cream cheese
1 tablespoon bourbon
¼ teaspoon salt
⅛ teaspoon hot pepper sauce or Tabasco
One 3¾ ounce can smoked oysters
¾ cup toasted almonds
¼ cup finely minced parsley

Combine all ingredients, except for parsley, in a food processor and process until oysters and almonds are coarsely chopped, and all ingredients are thoroughly combined.

Spoon into a 3-cup crock, sprinkle with chopped parsley, and chill for 2 to 4 hours.

Serves 4 to 6.

PÂTÉ POSTSCRIPT: TOASTING NUTS FOR PÂTÉS

WALNUTS: *Drop nuts into boiling water and cook for 3 minutes. Drain and place in a single layer on a flat baking pan. Toast for 15 minutes in a preheated 350° oven.*

ALMONDS: *Follow directions above, but remove almond skins after nuts have been boiled and drained.*

PÂTÉ OF GOLDEN CAVIAR FROM MIRASSOU WINERY

2 teaspoons unflavored gelatin
¼ cup white Burgundy or Pinot Blanc
2 hard-cooked eggs, finely chopped
½ cup homemade mayonnaise I (page 190)
1 shallot, grated
4 ounces Golden Caviar
2 teaspoons lemon juice
Freshly ground white pepper to taste
½ cup heavy sweet cream, whipped

Sprinkle gelatin over wine in a small saucepan and allow to sit for 10 minutes. Place over low heat until gelatin is dissolved and then set aside to cool.

Combine hard-cooked eggs, mayonnaise, shallot, caviar, and lemon juice. Add gelatin and blend well. Season with white pepper. Fold in whipped cream and spoon into a lightly oiled 1½-cup pâté mold.

Chill for 4 hours. Unmold onto lettuce leaves arranged on a platter. Serve with toast points and Mirassou champagne.

Serves 2 to 4.

TAPENADE

Make olive tapenade part of a party buffet, or serve before dinner with drinks. Serve with a crock of butter and a heaping basket of sliced French bread.

   6 fillets of anchovies with capers
   1 cup pitted black olives (California ripe olives), drained
   ¼ cup olive oil
   1 tablespoon lemon juice

Combine all ingredients in a food processor and process until finely chopped and thoroughly blended.

Yield: 1½ cups, approximately

PÂTÉ POSTSCRIPT: DEVILED EGG PÂTÉ

Deviled eggs too familiar? Prepare a crock of Deviled Egg Pâté instead: combine 6 hard-cooked eggs with ½ cup mayonnaise, 2 teaspoons Dijon mustard, and ⅛ teaspoon hot pepper sauce. Process in food processor with quick on and off pulsing. Spoon into a crock, garnish with chopped parsley or green onions (scallions), and chill before serving.

CHAPTER SIX

THE MAIN ATTRACTION

If you're building a dinner around a main pâté course, choose one of the heartier dishes: a pâté en croûte is fine, and a tourte or deep-dish pie will also be welcome. A gâteau de viandes or a meat-filled pâté pantin will make family and friends sit up and smile, while a salmon coulibiac is perfect for those evening parties when elegance does count.

When pâté is the main course at a simple dinner, consider a serving of hot, creamy soup—New England clam chowder or potage parmentier—as a first course. This is especially appropriate if you're serving a cold pâté. If the centerpiece pâté is hot, a cold vegetable dish—asparagus vinaigrette, for example—is a nice introduction to the meal.

The choice of dessert depends on the richness of the pâté. A light fish pâté can be followed by a meringue and cream dessert, while a tourte needs only a light sorbet or a few perfect strawberries or raspberries, with a touch of powdered sugar, to round out the meal.

VEAL AND CHICKEN TERRINE

1 shallot, finely chopped
1 clove garlic, finely chopped
4 tablespoons butter
1 pound veal, cubed
5 chicken legs, skinned and boned, the meat cut into
     pieces
1½ cups bread crumbs
1 egg
Salt and freshly ground black pepper to taste
½ teaspoon quatre-épices (page 211)
3 tablespoons chopped dill
½ cup dry white vermouth

Sauté shallot and garlic in butter, stirring, for 3 minutes. Reserve.

Using a food processor, coarsely grind veal and chicken.

Add shallot-garlic-butter to ground meats and blend in remaining ingredients until mixture is thoroughly combined.

Butter an 8-cup terrine or loaf pan and spoon meat mixture into terrine. Set terrine in a bain-marie and bake in a preheated 350° oven for 1½ hours. May be served hot or cold.

Serves 4 to 6.

TERRINE OF PORK AND RABBIT FROM THE DORDOGNE

2 pounds pork, thinly sliced
1 pound rabbit meat, sliced
2 shallots, chopped
1 clove garlic, chopped
¼ cup chopped parsley
Salt and freshly ground black pepper to taste
1 bay leaf
2 cups dry white wine
½ cup dry sherry
Slices of blanched bacon to line and cover terrine
2 black truffles, chopped (optional)

Combine pork, rabbit, shallots, garlic, parsley, salt, pepper, bay leaf, and white wine in a large bowl. Stir to mix and refrigerate for 24 hours.

Discard bay leaf. Remove half of pork and rabbit meat from bowl with a slotted spoon and, using a food processor, grind meats with sherry; correct seasoning.

Line a 3-quart terrine with bacon slices, allowing ends to hang over sides of terrine. Place half of ground meat in terrine, smooth over, and top with half of sliced meat. Cover with remainder of ground meat and place chopped truffles on top.

Place remainder of sliced meat on top, pressing down into ground meat. Cover with ends of bacon slices and with additional bacon slices so that terrine is completely covered.

Place terrine in a bain-marie in a preheated 350° oven and bake for 1½ hours. Weight and cool terrine. Refrigerate for 8 hours.

Serves 8 to 10.

TERRINE D'OIE AUX NOISETTES

½ pound pork liver, cubed
½ pound pork shoulder, cubed
Breast from uncooked goose, cubed (½ pound after re-
    moving skin and bones)
1 pound sliced bacon, blanched
2 eggs
2 tablespoons all-purpose flour
1 cup dry white wine
4 shallots, chopped
2 ounces whole filberts
Salt and freshly ground black pepper to taste
Aspic I (page 205)

Using a food processor, finely grind pork liver, pork shoulder, goose, and ½ pound of bacon. Mix thoroughly with remaining ingredients, except aspic and remaining bacon.

Line a 2-quart terrine with bacon slices. Spoon meat mixture into terrine. Cover and refrigerate overnight.

Next day, cover with lid or foil and place in a bain-marie. Bake in a preheated 350° oven for 2 hours. Uncover and pour ½ cup aspic over top. Cover and bake an additional 15 minutes. Cool for 30 minutes. Refrigerate, covered, for 24 hours.

Serves 6 to 8.

MIRASSOU WINERY'S LICHEE CHICKEN PÂTÉ

California wineries are interested in developing a cuisine that will complement their wines, and the following pâté is a fine example of their culinary imagination. Lichee fruit and Chinese Five-Spice Powder add a subtle oriental nuance to this dish.

1 16-ounce can whole lichees, drained
½ cup Chenin Blanc wine or other fruity dry white wine
2 shallots
1¼ pounds chicken breasts, skinned, boned, and cut into
    chunks (approximately 3 whole breasts)
1 cup heavy sweet cream (whipping cream)
1 cup finely crushed ice
Salt and freshly ground white pepper to taste
1¼ teaspoons Chinese Five-Spice Powder
1 green onion (scallion), finely chopped
3 egg whites, beaten until stiff
Butter
12–16 green, almond-stuffed olives
1 cup coarsely chopped water chestnuts
Cashew Cream Sauce (page 183)

Marinate drained lichees in wine and reserve.

Using a food processor, puree shallots and chicken until smooth. Spoon chicken mixture into a bowl and place in freezer until it is thoroughly chilled.

Return chicken puree to food processor and gradually add cream. Blend until cream is thoroughly incorporated into chicken mixture. Gradually add ice to chicken-cream mixture and continue processing until ice is incorporated into mixture. Add seasonings and green onion and process just to combine.

Spoon chicken mixture into a bowl and carefully fold in beaten egg whites. Place chicken mixture in freezer while preparing mold.

Butter an 8-cup pâté mold. Drain lichees and tuck an olive inside each lichee, allowing almond end to protrude. Arrange lichees olive side down around bottom of mold.

Spoon half of chicken mixture into bottom of mold, making sure spaces around the lichees are filled. Spread chopped water chestnuts evenly over chicken mixture and top with remaining chicken mixture. Smooth out top and tap sides of mold with knife handle to eliminate air bubbles.

Cover mold tightly with buttered foil and place in a bain-marie in a 350° preheated oven. Bake for 30 to 45 minutes, or until a knife inserted in center of pâté comes out clean.

Allow pâté to rest out of oven for 15 minutes before unmolding. Run a sharp knife around sides of mold and turn upside down over a serving platter. Serve with Cashew Cream Sauce.

Serves 6 to 8.

TERRINE OF FRESH DUCK LIVER PÂTÉ WITH PISTACHIO FROM FOURNOU'S OVENS

From the Stanford Court Hotel in San Francisco comes this recipe for their very special pâté. A rich mélange of duck livers and pork studded with pistachio nuts and truffles, the pâté is luxurious. It's best served with chilled champagne, and Jim Nassikas, owner of the Stanford Court, usually recommends a bottle of the bubbly from California. A dry white wine also makes fine company.

1 pound thinly sliced fatback to line and cover the terrine
2 slices white bread, processed into crumbs
¼ cup milk
1 pound duck livers
1 pound fatback
1 pound lean pork shoulder, cubed
1½ teaspoons salt, or to taste
½ teaspoon cinnamon
½ teaspoon ground allspice
¼ teaspoon nutmeg
⅛ teaspoon ground cloves
¼ teaspoon ground cardamom
½ teaspoon white pepper
1½ tablespoons all-purpose flour
4 tablespoons brandy
4 tablespoons pistachio nuts
1 tablespoon minced black truffle (optional)
2 teaspoons thyme
6 bay leaves

Line a 2-quart terrine or a 9×5×3-inch loaf pan with sliced fatback, so that the bottom and sides are completely covered. Let ends of fatback hang over sides of terrine.

Combine bread crumbs and milk in a small bowl. Mix and reserve.

Using a food processor, finely grind the duck livers, 1 pound fatback, and pork shoulder twice. Add bread crumb-milk combination, all seasonings (except thyme and bay leaves), flour, and brandy and continue processing until mixture is a smooth puree.

Correct seasoning, adding more salt, spices, or brandy if mixture is too bland.

Spoon meat mixture into a bowl and stir in pistachios and truffle, combining thoroughly.

Spoon mixture into terrine, patting down with hands to rid the mixture of air.

Fold fatback over top of pâté and smooth into a neat loaf. Sprinkle with thyme and place bay leaves in a row across the top.

Bake the terrine in a bain-marie in a preheated 375° oven for about 2 hours, or until a metal skewer inserted in the center and held for 10 seconds comes out hot. Terrine should have pulled away from sides of dish and juices should be yellow, not pink.

Remove terrine from oven. Discard top layer of fatback and bay leaves. Allow to cool. Weight and refrigerate for 8 hours. Allow pâté flavors to combine for 24 hours before serving.

Serves 10 to 12.

TERRINE OF CALF'S LIVER, FROM CZECHOSLOVAKIA

1 pound calf's liver
4 tablespoons rendered goose or chicken fat, or butter
3 medium onions, coarsely chopped
4 hard-cooked eggs
2 ounces cognac
Salt and freshly ground black pepper to taste

Wrap calf's liver in foil and bake in a 325° oven for 1 hour. Open foil and allow liver to remain in oven for an additional 5 minutes. Liver should be cooked so that it is pink inside, but not bloody.

Heat goose fat, chicken fat, or butter in a large skillet and sauté onions until they are translucent. Reserve.

Cut cooked calf's liver into large pieces and, using a food processor, grind liver with hard-cooked eggs. Add cognac and onions with juices from skillet to liver. Process thoroughly and season to taste. Spoon into a 1-quart terrine and refrigerate overnight.

Serves 4 to 6.

NEW YEAR'S DAY PORK PIE

If revelers are still in your house the day after the party, or if friends are coming over to watch a football game, it's smart to have this dish on hand, especially as it can be cooked in advance, frozen, and reheated when needed. The meat is marinated for two days, important to consider whenever you're planning to serve this dish.

1 (6-pound) pork shoulder roast, boned
2 packages whole pickling spices
2 onions, chopped
2 cloves garlic, chopped
1 large bunch of parsley, chopped
2 tablespoons salt, or to taste
½ teaspoon freshly ground black pepper
½ cup red wine vinegar
1 to 1½ fifths dry Chablis or white Burgundy
4½–5 cups all-purpose flour, sifted
1¼ teaspoons baking powder
1 teaspoon salt
8 tablespoons shortening
4 tablespoons butter
1½ cups milk
1 egg

Remove all fat from pork and cut meat into ½-inch cubes. Place in a large glass or porcelain bowl—do not use a metal bowl.

Combine pickling spices, onions, garlic, parsley, salt, pepper, and wine vinegar. Mix well and pour over meat, adding enough wine to cover. Marinate in refrigerator for 2 days.

Strain marinade from meat and reserve. Place meat in a strainer or colander and rinse off pickling spices. Return meat to marinade and marinate for an additional 4 to 6 hours.

Prepare pastry in a food processor by combining flour, baking powder, salt, shortening, and butter and processing until mixture forms coarse crumbs. Combine milk and egg and add gradually until mixture forms a ball.

Roll out two-thirds of the dough to fit a 9×13-inch baking pan. Line the pan with the dough, letting approximately 1½ inches of dough hang over the sides.

Spoon drained meat into pan, reserving the marinade. Spoon 1 cup of marinade over meat, reserving remainder of marinade.

Roll out remaining dough and cover the top of the pie. Fold overhanging dough from bottom crust over top crust, sealing edges carefully. You may use reserved marinade to help seal edges. Sprinkle ¼ cup marinade over top crust.

Cut a small hole in center of pie and pierce pastry with tines of a fork.

Bake pie in a preheated 325° oven for 1 hour, or until crust is golden brown.

Serves 8 to 10.

KING ARTHUR'S
SQUAB AND PORK PIE

According to To the King's Taste,* *a book on English medieval cookery, the nursery rhyme line "Four-and-twenty blackbirds baked in a pie . . ." was based on the custom of filling an empty baked pie shell with small live birds. A baked top crust covered the birds just before the pie was brought to the table, and then with one cut—gentle, we hope—the birds were released, flying up and out, twittering, singing, and entertaining the surprised guests.*

At the same time, the guests were served an edible pie that contained a combination of cooked small birds and pork, all heavily spiced. To the King's Taste *offers a recipe for this bird-and-pork pie, and the following is an adaptation of that idea.*

If you have a ceramic pie bird, use it when baking King Arthur's pie. Place the pie bird in the center of the pie, on top of the filling. The top crust holds the base of the bird secure, and the bird will act as a vent, allowing steam to escape. Recite "Four-and-twenty blackbirds baked in a pie . . ." when you bring this delicious dish to the table.

> **Pâte brisée II (page 23)**
> **2 tablespoons olive oil**
> **1 pound lean pork, cut into small cubes**
> **Salt and freshly ground black pepper to taste**
> **4 quail,† cut in half**
> **1 cup milk**
> **½–1 cup all-purpose flour**
> **1 tablespoon olive oil**

---

* *To the King's Taste,* Lorna J. Sass, The Metropolitan Museum of Art, New York, 1975.
† 1 squab or 1 small rock cornish hen, cut into quarters may substitute for quail.

---

1 tablespoon butter
2 cups beef broth
½ cup white raisins
2 apples, cored and sliced
1 tablespoon dark brown sugar
½ teaspoon ground ginger
¼ teaspoon ground cinnamon
2 tablespoons butter

A conventional pie pan is too shallow for King Arthur's pie. Use an 8-cup oval baking dish, casserole, or terrine with a depth of 2–3 inches, or use a deep-dish pie pan. Line pan with pâte brisée pastry and partially bake bottom crust.

Heat 2 tablespoons oil in a large skillet and sauté pork until lightly brown on all sides. Using a slotted spoon, transfer pork to a large bowl, season, and reserve.

Dip pieces of quail into milk, dredge with flour, and season.

Heat 1 tablespoon oil and 1 tablespoon butter in a skillet and sauté quail until brown. Remove from heat and drain on paper towels. Reserve.

Heat beef broth to a simmer and add raisins. Simmer for 5 minutes and stir in all remaining ingredients, except for 2 tablespoons butter. Cook, stirring, for 2 minutes, or until all ingredients are thoroughly combined. Pour beef sauce mixture over pork cubes and stir to combine.

Place pieces of quail in pastry shell and spoon pork and sauce over and around quail.

Roll out remaining pastry and cover filling with top crust. Seal edges. Cut hole in center of pastry to allow steam to escape, or use a ceramic pie bird.

Dot crust with butter and bake pie in a preheated 350° oven for 1¼ hours.

Serves 6.

SAUSAGE PÂTÉ IN PASTRY CRUST

1 small onion
1 clove garlic
2 green onions (scallions), each one cut into 3 pieces
6 slices bacon
2 pounds pork sausage meat
3 eggs
3 cups bread crumbs
Salt and freshly ground black pepper to taste
¼ teaspoon cardamom
2 tablespoons brandy
Butter
Pâte brisée I (page 22)
1 beaten egg

Using a food processor, chop onion, garlic, and green onions.
Leave vegetables in processor.

microwave is better

In a large skillet, fry the bacon. When bacon is crisp, remove
from heat and combine with sausage meat. Add bacon, sausage
meat, 3 eggs, and bread crumbs to food processor. Process to
combine thoroughly. Season sausage mixture and add brandy.
Butter a 5-cup terrine or loaf pan. Line with pâte brisée, pressing it firmly against the sides and bottom of dish. Spoon meat
mixture into terrine. Top mixture with pastry and seal edges.
Brush with beaten egg.

Bake terrine in a preheated 350° oven for 45 minutes. Refrigerate overnight. Serve from terrine, or unmold.

Serves 8.

WERNER ALBRECHT'S DEEP-DISH RABBIT PIE

Werner Albrecht is the Swiss chef who presides so deliciously over the restaurants in San Francisco's Four Seasons Clift Hotel. This Rabbit Pie is one of Werner's most popular dishes, and it's easy to prepare. Many supermarkets around the country carry frozen rabbit, cut into serving pieces, and a number of ethnic meat markets—both Italian and French—carry fresh rabbit, as well.

1 rabbit, cut into serving pieces
2 cups dry white wine
½ teaspoon salt
¼ teaspoon freshly ground black pepper
1 onion, thinly sliced
1 clove garlic, pressed
1 bay leaf
4–6 tablespoons all-purpose flour
4 tablespoons butter
2 cups chicken broth
1 onion, chopped
4 carrots, sliced into rounds
2 potatoes, cubed
1 tablespoon butter
1 tablespoon all-purpose flour

Ingredients for Pastry:

2 cups all-purpose flour
¼ pound plus 2 tablespoons butter
1 egg
1 teaspoon salt
1½–2 tablespoons ice water

Marinate rabbit in wine, to which you've added the salt, pepper, sliced onion, garlic, and bay leaf, for 1 day. Strain, discard onion and bay leaf, and reserve marinade. Dry rabbit pieces. Dredge rabbit pieces in flour.

Melt 4 tablespoons butter in a deep skillet and brown pieces of meat. Add marinade and chicken broth and simmer, covered, until rabbit is almost tender, about 1 hour. Add chopped onion, carrots and potatoes to skillet and cook an additional 30 minutes, covered.

Prepare a beurre manié by working 1 tablespoon butter and 1 tablespoon flour into a paste. Blend with sauce in skillet and simmer, stirring from time to time, until sauce thickens. Place rabbit in a 2-quart terrine or deep casserole, spoon sauce and vegetables over rabbit, and reserve.

Prepare pastry in a food processor by combining flour, butter, egg, and salt, and processing until mixture forms coarse crumbs. Gradually add ice water until mixture forms a ball.

Roll out dough, and cover top of baking dish. Seal dough to edge of dish and make several slits in crust.

Bake in a preheated 400° oven for 30 minutes, or until crust is brown.

Serves 4 to 5.

PÂTÉ PANTIN

4 tablespoons butter
5 large onions, chopped
1 cup chicken broth
Salt and freshly ground black pepper to taste
¼ teaspoon grated nutmeg
1 pound mushrooms, cut into large pieces
1 cup milk
⅓ cup heavy sweet cream (whipping cream)
1 egg
1 tablespoon all-purpose flour
½ cup toasted, chopped almonds
¼ pound boiled ham, diced
½ cup chopped parsley
½ teaspoon dried tarragon
Pâte brisée II (page 23)
Butter
2 cups cooked brown rice
1 egg yolk

Heat butter in a large skillet. Sauté the onions until just translucent. Add the broth, salt, pepper, and nutmeg, and simmer until onions are tender and broth has been absorbed.

While onions are cooking, simmer the mushrooms in milk until mushrooms are tender and have absorbed the milk. Season to taste.

Combine onions, cream, egg, and flour in a food processor and process until thoroughly combined. Spoon cream-onion puree into skillet and cook, stirring, over low heat until mixture thickens. Cool for 5 minutes and stir in mushrooms, almonds, and ham. Add parsley and tarragon, and correct seasoning.

Roll out pâte brisée pastry into a rectangle, approximately 12× 24 inches. Carefully place pastry on a buttered baking sheet.

Spoon half the rice onto half of the pastry, leaving a 1-inch border. Spoon onion-mushroom-ham mixture onto rice and top with a layer of remaining rice.

Fold pastry over filling and seal the three sides carefully. Brush pastry with egg yolk and make a hole in the center of the crust. Prick pastry with fork.

Bake in a preheated 375° oven for 30 minutes, or until pastry is golden brown. Cool for 15 minutes before cutting and serving.

Serves 6 to 8.

Make sure mixture is not too wet - cook without lids on pans

Dish is essentially pasta with mushroom flavor

PÂTÉ PANTIN
WITH ASPIC

*Another version of the rectangular pâté pantin, made with pork
and sausage and finished with an aspic.*

> ½ **pound pork, cubed**
> ¼ **pound fatback, cubed**
> ¼ **pound pork sausage meat**
> 1 **egg**
> **Salt and freshly ground black pepper to taste**
> ¼ **teaspoon mace**
> **Pinch of cloves**
> ⅛ **teaspoon thyme**
> ¼ **cup Madeira**
> **Pâte brisée II (page 23)**
> **Butter**
> 1 **egg**
> 1 **tablespoon milk**
> **Aspic I (page 205)**

Using a food processor, grind pork with fatback. Add sausage
meat, 1 egg, seasonings, and Madeira and process until completely combined.

Roll out pâte brisée into a rectangle, about 12×24 inches, and
carefully place pastry on a buttered baking sheet. Place meat
mixture in center of one half of rectangle of pastry, leaving a
2-inch border on all sides. Bring other half of pastry rectangle
over filled half, sealing edges carefully.

Beat egg with milk and brush over pastry. Cut a hole in center
of pastry and pierce pastry with a fork. Bake pâté in a preheated 375° oven for 10 minutes. Reduce heat to 350° and
bake an additional 50 to 60 minutes, or until pastry is brown. If

---

pastry browns too quickly, cover with foil, leaving vent hole open.

Allow pâté to cool and refrigerate for 8 hours. Prepare aspic and, using a funnel or baster, pour aspic into pâté through center hole in pastry. Gently tip the pâté from side to side, so that the aspic will completely cover meat. Refrigerate pâté for 4 hours, so that aspic will set.

Remove from refrigerator 30 minutes before serving.

Serves 4 to 6.

VEAL AND CHICKEN PÂTÉ IN CRUST

¾ pound veal, cubed
¾ pound boned, skinned chicken, cubed
½ cup bread crumbs
1 egg
¼ cup heavy sweet cream (whipping cream)
2 tablespoons dry vermouth
¼ pound mushrooms, finely chopped
¼ teaspoon Herbes de Provence
1 tablespoon chopped parsley
Salt and freshly ground black pepper to taste
Pâte brisée I (page 22)
1 egg, beaten

Using a food processor, grind veal and chicken. Spoon meat into a bowl and add all other ingredients, except for pâte brisée and beaten egg. Mix thoroughly.

Spoon meat mixture into a buttered 9×5×3-inch loaf pan. Bake in a preheated 350° oven for 1 hour. Allow meat mixture to cool and then unmold.

Roll out pâte brisée and place cooled meat in center. Fold dough over the meat to cover it completely. Tuck in dough at the edges. Place seam side down on a baking sheet. Decorate top with scraps of dough. Cut a small hole in center of pastry and prick dough casing with a fork at the edges of the pâté.

Brush dough with beaten egg and bake in a preheated 400° oven for approximately 30 minutes, or until crust is brown.

Serves 8.

TOURTE OF PORK WITH ONIONS, FROM ALSACE

4 tablespoons butter
1 large onion, finely chopped
2 cloves garlic, minced
1½ pounds pork, cubed
4 slices white bread or French bread
Warm water
1 egg
Salt and freshly ground white pepper
¼ teaspoon nutmeg
8 tablespoons cognac
Butter
Pâte brisée II (page 23)
1 egg, beaten
½ cup crème fraîche (page 210)

Heat butter in a skillet and sauté onion and garlic until translucent. Spoon into a bowl.

Using a food processor, chop pork coarsely and add to onion-garlic mixture.

Soak bread in warm water until just softened. Squeeze out excess water, and add bread to pork-onion mixture. Add 1 egg, seasonings, and cognac and mix until thoroughly combined.

Line a buttered deep-dish pie plate, or a 2-quart tourtière or casserole, with pâte brisée pastry dough. Spoon in meat mixture and cover with a top crust of pastry dough. Seal edges carefully. Cut a small hole in the center of the pastry and brush pastry with beaten egg.

Bake tourte in a preheated 400° oven for 20 minutes. Turn heat down to 350° and bake for another 30 to 40 minutes, or until crust is brown.

Before serving, using a funnel or baster, gradually pour crème fraîche into tourte through hole in center of pastry.

Serves 4.

TOURTE DE POULET BERGERAC

Two 3-pound chickens, poached
Poaching liquid
3 shallots, minced
¼ cup minced parsley
½ teaspoon quatre-épices (page 211)
3 eggs
3 cups heavy sweet cream (whipping cream)
Salt and freshly ground white pepper to taste
Butter
Pâte brisée I, doubled (page 22)

Bone and skin poached chickens, discarding bone and skin. Reserve liquid. Cut chicken meat into large pieces and reserve.

Strain poaching liquid into a large saucepan and stir in shallots, parsley, and quatre-épices.

Combine eggs and heavy cream in a bowl, mixing just to combine. Over very low heat, gradually add egg-cream mixture to poaching liquid, stirring. Mixture should not cook. When sauce is well blended, add chicken pieces and stir to combine. Season to taste.

Butter a 10-inch tourtière, deep-dish pie pan, or ovenproof casserole and line with pâte brisée. Spoon chicken-sauce mixture onto dough and cover with a top crust. Seal edges. Cut a small hole in the center and prick pastry with a fork.

Bake in a preheated 400° oven for 40 minutes, or until crust is brown.

Serves 6 to 8.

VEAL TOURTE FROM NORMANDY

1 pound veal, finely diced
1 cup dry white wine
1 ounce calvados or apple brandy
2 cloves garlic, minced
2 stalks celery, finely chopped
Salt to taste
¼ teaspoon quatre-épices (page 211)
Butter
Pâte brisée I, doubled (page 22)
1 medium apple, peeled and thinly sliced
3 eggs, lightly beaten
2 cups heavy sweet cream (whipping cream)

In a large bowl, combine veal, wine, calvados or apple brandy, garlic, celery, salt, and quatre-épices. Cover and refrigerate for 8 hours.

Line a buttered deep-dish pie plate, or a 2-quart tourtière or casserole, with pâte brisée. Using a slotted spoon, remove meat from marinade and spoon onto pastry. Top with apple slices. Cover meat and apple with top crust and seal edges of pastry carefully. Cut a small hole in center of pastry.

Bake tourte in a preheated 400° oven for 30 minutes.

Combine eggs and cream and beat until just combined. Remove tourte from oven and, using a funnel or a baster, gradually pour egg-cream mixture into pie through hole in center of pastry.

Lower oven temperature to 350° and continue baking tourte for an additional 30 minutes.

Serves 4.

TOURTE DE JAMBON

1¼ cups all-purpose flour
¼ cup cornmeal
¼ pound plus 4 tablespoons butter (12 tablespoons in all)
4 tablespoons milk
4 tablespoons butter
2 cups finely chopped roast fresh ham, pork, or baked ham
1 medium onion, chopped
2 eggs, beaten
¾ cup sour cream
Salt and freshly ground black pepper to taste
1 teaspoon chopped chives
¼ teaspoon caraway seed
1 egg yolk, beaten

Using a food processor, combine flour, cornmeal, and ¼ pound plus 4 tablespoons butter. Process until mixture forms coarse crumbs. Add milk gradually until mixture forms a ball. Refrigerate for 30 minutes before using.

Roll out pastry and fit into a 9-inch pie pan. Partially bake in a preheated 425° oven for 10 minutes.

Heat 4 tablespoons butter in a large skillet. Add ham or pork and cook, stirring, until meat is brown. Add onion and cook until wilted.

Spoon ingredients from skillet into a large bowl. Add all other ingredients, except beaten egg yolk, and mix thoroughly. Spoon ham mixture into partially baked pie shell and cover with remaining pastry. Seal edges. Brush with egg yolk and cut a small hole in center of pastry. Bake in a preheated 350° oven for 30 minutes, or until crust is brown.

Serves 4 to 6.

CHICKEN AND SWEETBREAD TOURTE

1 pair sweetbreads
6 tablespoons butter
1 tablespoon lemon juice
½ cup diced boiled ham
½ pound mushrooms, sliced
One 2½-pound chicken roasted, with pan juices
1 ounce brandy
1 ounce port wine
2 cups heavy sweet cream (whipping cream)
Salt and freshly ground white pepper to taste
Pâte brisée I (page 22)

Soak sweetbreads in cold water for 1 hour, drain. Cook sweetbreads in water until they become white, about 20 minutes. Drain, allow to cool, and remove skin and connective tubes. Slice the sweetbreads.

Heat butter in a large skillet and stir in lemon juice. Add sweetbreads, ham, and mushrooms to skillet and cook for 5 minutes over low heat, stirring. Reserve.

Cut chicken into 8 pieces and place chicken pieces and juices from the pan in which the chicken was roasted into a 3-quart terrine, tourtière, or deep-dish pie plate.

Combine brandy, port, and cream in a saucepan. Heat, stirring, until just lukewarm and blended, and pour over sweetbread mixture. Cook, stirring, over low heat for 3 minutes.

Spoon sweetbread-sauce mixture over chicken. Season and cover with pâte brisée. Seal edges. Cut 3 or 4 slashes in pastry and bake tourte in a 400° oven for 30 minutes, or until crust is brown.

Serves 6 to 8.

PÂTÉ DE POULET
À LA SENLIS

Senlis is a twelfth-century town about half an hour's drive outside of Paris. The town is frequently used as background in French historical films. The people of Senlis are proud of their ancient, well-kept streets, their venerable cathedral of Nôtre Dame, and their traditional chicken pie in a pâte brisée crust, which they prepare in a hinged pâté mold.

> One 3–3½ pound chicken
> 1 pound fresh pork, cubed
> 1 pound salt pork
> Liver of chicken
> ¼ teaspoon freshly ground white pepper
> Butter
> Pâte brisée II (page 23)
> 4 strips bacon, blanched
> ½ cup chicken broth
> ½ cup dry white vermouth
> 1 egg yolk, beaten

Bone breast of chicken, remove and discard skin, and cut meat into four slices.

Bone remainder of chicken and discard skin. Using a food processor, grind all chicken, except for breast meat, and spoon into a large bowl. Grind fresh pork and salt pork and add to ground chicken. Mix ground meats thoroughly. Dice chicken liver and stir into ground meats. Season with pepper, and reserve.

Butter a hinged 12- or 14-inch pâté mold or a casserole and line with pastry, pressing it against bottom and sides of mold. Allow pastry to hang over the edges by 1 inch. Place 2 strips of bacon lengthwise on pastry. Cover with half the ground meat mixture and top with 2 slices of chicken.

Cover chicken slices with remainder of ground meat mixture. Top with remaining 2 slices of chicken, and finish with remaining 2 strips of bacon. Combine broth and vermouth in a bowl, mix well, and pour over assembled pâté.

Roll out pastry to form top crust and fit on top of pâté. Seal edges and brush with beaten egg yolk. Cut a small hole in center of crust and bake in a preheated 350° oven for 1½ hours. If pastry becomes brown too soon, cover pâté with foil, making sure that center hole remains uncovered so that steam can escape.

Allow pâté to cool before removing sides of the mold.

Serves 8 to 10.

PÂTÉ DE POULET ET SAUCISSE

4 tablespoons butter
1 tablespoon olive oil
3 breasts of chicken, boned, skin removed, cut into 9
   pieces (approximately 1½–2 pounds)
Salt and freshly ground black pepper
¼ pound pork sausage meat
¼ pound chicken livers
2 tablespoons butter
Pâte brisée I, doubled (page 22)
2 cups chicken broth
4 tablespoons butter
1 cup dry white wine
1 tablespoon chopped parsley
2 green onions (scallions), chopped

Heat 4 tablespoons butter and the oil in a large skillet; sauté chicken pieces in skillet until lightly brown, turning frequently. Do not overcook, or chicken will become dry. Season with salt and pepper and reserve chicken in skillet.

Using a food processor, grind sausage meat with chicken livers and combine thoroughly. Form sausage-liver mixture into small meatballs and brown in 2 tablespoons butter in another skillet. Reserve.

Line a deep-dish pie plate or a casserole with pastry. Using a slotted spoon, remove chicken pieces from skillet and place into pie plate. Scatter sausage-liver meatballs over and around chicken pieces.

Pour 1 cup of chicken broth into skillet in which chicken cooked.

Heat, stirring, and combine with juices in skillet. When mixture has come to a simmer, pour over meats in pie plate.

Cover pie with pastry, sealing edges. Cut a small hole in center of pastry and bake pâté in a preheated 350° oven for 30 minutes, or until pastry is brown.

While pâté bakes, combine remaining cup of chicken broth, 4 tablespoons butter, white wine, parsley, and green onions in a saucepan. Bring to a simmer and cook until mixture reduces by half. Pour into a sauce boat and serve with pâté.

Serves 4 to 6.

TRADITIONAL EASTER PIE FROM THE BERRY REGION OF FRANCE

2 pounds pork, cubed
1 pound veal, cubed
2 tablespoons chopped fresh parsley
1 large onion
Salt and freshly ground black pepper to taste
Pâte brisée II (page 23)
Hard-cooked eggs, halved lengthwise
Butter
¼ teaspoon nutmeg
¼ teaspoon thyme
1 egg, beaten

Using a food processor, grind pork and veal with parsley, onion, and salt and pepper.

Roll out half of pastry into a large circle and place on a buttered baking sheet.

Spoon half of meat mixture in center of pastry circle, leaving a 2-inch border. Place hard-cooked egg halves on meat, dot with butter, and season with nutmeg and thyme. Top with remaining meat mixture.

Cover pâté with remaining pastry, bring up sides of bottom crust, and seal edges carefully. Brush top and sides of pastry with beaten egg and cut a small hole in center of pastry. Prick pastry with tines of a fork.

Bake in a preheated 325° oven for 2 hours.

Serves 10 to 12.

PETITS PAINS DE VIANDES

From France comes this recipe for individual pâtés that are shaped like tiny loaves. Hence the name—little meat breads. They may be shaped by hand—a round little loaf is especially appealing—and baked in a shallow baking pan, or they may be baked in individual soufflé dishes and then unmolded. Petits Pains de Viandes are easy to prepare, can be made in advance, are good hot or cold, and are an interesting change from the usual hamburger.

    1 tablespoon vegetable oil
    1 small onion, minced
    1 small green pepper, finely chopped
    1 clove garlic, pressed
    1 pound beef, cubed
    ½ pound pork, cubed
    1 cup bread crumbs
    1 egg, beaten
    ½ cup heavy sweet cream (whipping cream)
    Salt and freshly ground black pepper to taste
    ¼ teaspoon ground cumin
    Tomato Sauce Provençal (page 183)

Heat oil in a large skillet and sauté onion, green pepper, and garlic until onion is translucent. Reserve.

Using a food processor, coarsely grind beef and pork and add to skillet. Add all other ingredients, except for Tomato Sauce Provençal, and mix thoroughly.

Shape meat into four individual round loaves, or spoon each portion into a 1½-cup soufflé mold. Place Petits Pains de Viandes in a shallow baking dish and bake in a preheated 400°

oven for 30 minutes. (If using soufflé dishes place them directly in the oven and allow to cool for 5 minutes before unmolding.)

Serve hot with Tomato Sauce Provençal, or serve cold.

Serves 4.

INDIVIDUAL QUAIL
PÂTÉS IN PASTRY

*When giving an elegant dinner party serve each of your guests an
individual pâté of boned quail and ham wrapped in a crust.*

> **6 tablespoons butter**
> **3 quail**
> **¼ pound chicken livers**
> **¼ pound pork, cut into small cubes**
> **1 egg yolk**
> **1 shallot**
> **2 tablespoons brandy**
> **Salt and freshly ground black pepper to taste**
> **6–10 slices boiled ham**
> **Pâte brisée I (page 22)**
> **1 egg, lightly beaten**
> **Butter**
> **Sauce Champignon (page 204)**

Heat butter in a large skillet and sauté quail, turning them
from side to side until they are lightly brown all over. Remove
birds from skillet and allow to cool until they can be easily
handled.

Cut birds in half and bone breast meat from each half. You
will now have 6 scallops of breast meat. Cut each of these 6
pieces in half. Bone thighs and second joints and reserve meat
separately from breast meat.

Combine chicken livers, pork, egg yolk, shallot, brandy, and
seasonings in a food processor and grind.

Place ham on a board. If ham slices are small, place 1 slice
overlapping another to make 6 portions of ham. Place 1 piece
of breast of quail on each portion of ham. Top with one-sixth
of ground meat mixture. Add one portion of thigh and second

joint meat and top with another piece of breast meat. Fold ham slice over meat filling. Repeat with all of ham portions and remainder of quail.

Roll out pâte brisée on a floured board and cut pastry into 6 rectangles. Each rectangle should be large enough to completely wrap around a ham roll.

Place a ham roll on each rectangle. Fold short ends of pastry in and fold long sides of pastry over them, carefully sealing all seams. Repeat with all ham rolls and pastry. Brush pastry-wrapped pâtés with beaten egg. Turn over and brush with remaining beaten egg. Cut a small hole in center of pastry of each pâté.

Place pâtés on a buttered baking dish and bake in a preheated 400° oven for 10 minutes. Reduce heat to 350° and continue baking for an additional 30 to 40 minutes, or until pastry is brown. If pastry seems to be browning too quickly, cover with foil, making sure that vent holes are left open.

Serve individual quail pâtés hot or cold with Sauce Champignon.

Serves 6.

GALANTINE OF PHEASANT À LA ANDRÉ MERCIER

The most glamorous dish in the pâté family is a galantine—boned poultry, stuffed with a meat mixture, cooked, and then decorated with aspic. And among galantines, the most elegant is a galantine of pheasant. The following recipe was developed by André Mercier, restaurant owner, chef, and food consultant.

> 2 pheasants, about 2½ pounds each, boned
> Slices of breast meat from pheasants
> ½ pound boiled ham, cut into long strips
> Livers of pheasants, each liver cut in half
> ½ pound fatback, cut into long strips
> ½ pound tongue, cut into julienne strips
> 3 ounces brandy
> Salt and freshly ground white pepper to taste
> ⅛ teaspoon thyme
> ½ pound veal, cubed
> ½ pound lean pork, cubed
> 2 eggs, lightly beaten
> 2 ounces pistachio nuts
> 2 ounces truffles, thinly sliced (optional)
> 2 quarts chicken stock or broth
> Chaud-Froid Sauce (page 207)
> Aspic I or II (page 205 or 206)

Spread out pheasant skins in a shallow pan, skin side down, and reserve.

Cut breast meat into long strips and combine in a bowl with half of ham, livers, half of fatback, and half of tongue. Add brandy, salt, pepper, and thyme. Mix to combine.

Divide this mixture in half and spoon each half onto a pheasant skin. Fold legs, wings, and skin over this stuffing. Cover pan with foil, and refrigerate for 24 hours.

Using a food processor, grind remaining ham, fatback, and tongue with remaining pheasant meat, the veal and pork. Add eggs, season, and mix thoroughly. Stir in pistachio nuts and truffles and mix to combine. Refrigerate overnight.

Remove pheasant skins from refrigerator and scrape breast meat stuffing from skins into a large bowl. Spoon a quarter of the ground meat mixture onto each pheasant skin. Top with half the stuffing and remainder of ground meat mixture.

Close galantines carefully, drawing sides of skin over stuffing. Sew skin together and fold neck flap over, sewing in place.

Adjust wings and drumsticks to form birdlike shape.

Wrap pheasants tightly in several layers of cheesecloth. Tie ends.

Heat chicken stock or broth and allow to simmer for 10 minutes. Place pheasants in stock and cook at a simmer for 1 hour; allow to cool in stock. Place pheasants in a pan. Strain stock and pour over pheasants. Cover tightly, place a weight on cover, and refrigerate overnight.

The next day lift pheasants out of stock—save stock for Chaud-Froid Sauce and aspic. Unwrap pheasants carefully and remove as much of sewing thread as possible. (Some of it may have to be removed when you slice the galantine.)

Use stock to prepare chaud-froid and aspic to glaze and decorate the galantine.

Brush or spoon a thin layer of chaud-froid over pheasants. Refrigerate until chaud-froid jells. Brush on another layer and refrigerate once again. Continue until the galantine is completely masked by sauce. Place galantine on a platter and garnish with chopped aspic. Slice and serve.

Serves 12 to 14.

GALANTINE OF CHICKEN

One 5-pound chicken, boned, bones reserved
Salt and freshly ground white pepper
1¼ pounds lean pork, diced
½ pound boiled ham, diced
¼ pound bacon, finely chopped
Liver from chicken
Salt and freshly ground white pepper to taste
¼ teaspoon quatre-épices (page 211)
1 tablespoon brandy
¼ cup dry vermouth
1 pound pork sausage meat
1 carrot, sliced
1 large onion, sliced
1 cup dry white wine
2 quarts chicken stock or broth
Bouquet garni: parsley, bay leaf, 1 clove garlic
Aspic I or II (page 205 or 206)

Place boned chicken skin side down on a board and season with salt and pepper. Reserve.

In a bowl, combine pork, ham, bacon, and liver from chicken. Add small pieces of meat from chicken that were cut out when chicken was boned. Season with salt, pepper, and quatre-épices. Add brandy and vermouth. Toss and allow to sit for 15 minutes. Spoon sausage meat onto the chicken and top with other combined meats. Tuck in ends of chicken skin and sew skin in the center. Tie chicken firmly in cheesecloth, making sure ends are tied.

Place carrot and onion slices in the bottom of a large Dutch oven or casserole. Add chicken bones. Place galantine on top and add wine, stock, and bouquet garni to pot.

Bring to a simmer and cook over low heat for 2 hours. Allow the galantine to cool in stock and refrigerate overnight, covered and weighted.

The next day remove galantine from stock. Reserve stock for aspic. Remove cheesecloth and all visible sewing threads. (You may have to remove remainder of threads when slicing galantine.) Prepare aspic.*

Brush a layer of aspic over galantine and chill until set. Brush another layer of aspic over galantine and chill again until aspic sets. Chill remaining aspic and cut into small cubes or diamonds. Spoon pieces of aspic onto a serving platter and place galantine on top.

Serves 10 to 12.

---

* *Note on aspic:* Because the bones of the chicken have simmered with the galantine, you may be able to make an aspic without using additional gelatin. If stock has gelatinized by morning, skim off top layer of fat and heat stock. Cook for 30 minutes until stock is reduced and allow to cool. Strain, cool again, and use as aspic.

PÂTÉ POSTSCRIPT: POACHED FISH

2 tablespoons butter
1 small onion, chopped
2 stalks celery, chopped
1 cup dry white wine
1 quart water
8 sprigs parsley, tied together
1 bay leaf
Salt to taste
4 whole peppercorns
Fillets of fish

Heat butter in a large, deep skillet. Sauté onion and celery until vegetables are translucent. Add wine and all other ingredients, except fish, to skillet.

Bring mixture to a boil, reduce heat, and simmer for 5 minutes.

Carefully place fish fillets in simmering liquid. Cover and cook over low heat, just until fish flakes.

Remove fish from liquid. Strain and reserve liquid for fish stock or sauces.

COULIBIAC DE SAUMON

Coulibiac of salmon is found on the menus of the most elegant—and expensive—restaurants around the world. It's a favorite in Paris and is often served at lavish dinner parties—usually provided by such outstanding caterers as Gaston Le Notre.

According to the excellent French encyclopedia on food, the Larousse Gastronomique, *the coulibiac is based on a hot fish pie from Russia, where it was made with salmon combined with sterlet, a small sturgeon that provides the best caviar.*

In nineteenth-century Paris, where the dish first became popular and where sterlet was not all that readily available, the salmon was combined with turbot, a distant relative of American halibut, and the kasha, or buckwheat groats originally called for, was replaced with rice.

By now, the idea of using two fish in a coulibiac has been mostly forgotten, and the coulibiac is generally prepared only with salmon. It is still prepared in the shape of the large rectangular pâté of France, the pantin.

> 2 cups fish stock or cold water
> 1 cup rice
> 1 tablespoon butter
> 1 small onion, finely chopped
> 4 tablespoons minced fresh dill
> Salt and freshly ground white pepper to taste
> 1½-pound fillet of salmon
> 2 cups dry white wine or fish stock
> 6 tablespoons butter
> 2 tablespoons all-purpose flour
> 1 pound mushrooms, thinly sliced
> 1 cup dry vermouth

½ cup heavy sweet cream (whipping cream)
½ cup Hollandaise Sauce (page 198)
4 tablespoons minced fresh parsley
Brioche pastry dough (page 24)
Crêpes with Dill (page 212)
4 hard-cooked eggs, sliced
2 egg yolks, lightly beaten
Butter
Beurre Blanc Sauce II (page 184)

Combine fish stock or water with rice in a large saucepan. Bring to a boil, stir, lower heat, and cover. Cook for 15 to 20 minutes, or until rice is tender and liquid is absorbed.

Heat 1 tablespoon butter in a skillet and sauté onion until translucent. Add dill and sauté another minute, stirring. Add onion-dill mixture to rice, stir to combine, and season to taste. Reserve.

Poach the salmon in white wine or fish stock. Fish will be cooked when it just flakes. Remove salmon to a platter and transfer poaching liquid to a saucepan. Cook until it is reduced by half. Reserve.

Heat 2 tablespoons of butter in a large saucepan, add flour, and cook this roux, stirring, until flour loses its raw color—about 3 minutes. Beat in reduced poaching liquid and cook, stirring, for 10 minutes. Reserve this fish sauce.

Heat 4 tablespoons butter in a skillet and sauté mushrooms, stirring, for 5 minutes. Add vermouth and cook, stirring, until liquid is reduced by half. Stir in cream and continue cooking until mixture thickens slightly.

Remove mushroom-cream mixture from heat and stir in fish sauce, mixing well. Add hollandaise and parsley and mix to combine. Reserve.

Place a floured pastry cloth on a board and roll out brioche pastry into a rectangle that's approximately 18×22 inches.

Assembling the Coulibiac:

Place 6 or 8 Crêpes with Dill on brioche dough, leaving a 4-inch border on all sides. Spoon half the rice mixture over the crêpes, leaving a 2-inch border on all sides. Place half the egg slices over rice mixture. Spoon half the mushroom-cream mixture over egg slices. Using a fork, break salmon into pieces and place on top of mushroom-cream layer.

Spoon remaining mushroom-cream layer over salmon. Top with remaining egg slices. Finish with remaining rice mixture. Top rice mixture with all remaining Crêpes with Dill.

Fold edges of bottom crêpes over the filling and tuck edges of the top layer of crêpes around the filling.

Brush the edges of the dough with beaten egg yolks. Fold long sides of dough over filling, then fold short ends over. Brush edges of pastry with egg and seal.

Carefully transfer coulibiac to a buttered baking sheet, seam side down. Brush with remaining beaten egg and garnish with leftover pastry scraps.

Cut 2 holes in pastry and pierce pastry with a fork.

Bake coulibiac in a preheated 400° oven for 10 minutes. Reduce heat to 350° and bake for another 20 to 30 minutes, or until pastry is brown.

Allow coulibiac to cool for 10 minutes before slicing.

Serve with Beurre Blanc Sauce.

Serves 12 to 14.

COULIBIAC OF SALMON, IN THE RUSSIAN MANNER

4 tablespoons butter
1 small onion, chopped
2 shallots, minced
½ pound mushrooms, sliced
½ cup sour cream
1 pound fillet of salmon, poached (page 109), poaching
    liquid reserved
1 pound fillet of sole, poached (page 109), poaching liq-
    uid reserved
3 tablespoons chopped parsley
2 tablespoons chopped dill
3 cups cooked kasha (buckwheat groats)
Salt and freshly ground black pepper to taste
4 hard-cooked eggs, chopped
Brioche pastry dough (page 24)
2 eggs, lightly beaten
Butter
Caviar Sauce (page 199)

Heat butter in a skillet. Sauté onion, shallots, and mushrooms in butter, stirring, until onion is translucent and mushrooms have released most of their liquid—about 3 minutes. Allow mixture to cool. Stir in sour cream. Mix well, and reserve.

Transfer liquid in which fish has poached to a saucepan.

Add parsley and dill and cook until mixture reduces to ½ cup. Stir liquid into kasha and combine. Season to taste. Reserve.

Using a fork, separate poached salmon and sole into large pieces and combine. Reserve.

Spread a floured pastry cloth on a board and roll out brioche dough into a rectangle about 18 × 20 inches.

Assembling the Coulibiac:

Spoon out half the kasha onto half the rectangle of dough, leaving a 3-inch border on all three sides.

Top kasha with half the chopped eggs.

Top eggs with half the mushroom-cream mixture.

Top mushroom cream mixture with all of fish. Add remaining mushroom-cream mixture. Add remaining chopped eggs. Add remaining kasha.

Using the cloth, lift unfilled half of dough over half with filling and cover. Seal the three edges. Brush pastry with beaten eggs and carefully transfer coulibiac to a buttered baking pan.

Cut 2 holes in pastry and pierce pastry with a fork.

Bake coulibiac in a preheated 400° oven for 10 minutes. Reduce heat to 350° and bake for another 20 to 30 minutes, or until pastry is brown.

Allow coulibiac to cool before slicing.

Serve with Caviar Sauce.

Serves 12.

PÂTÉ POSTSCRIPT: CHICKEN COULIBIAC

In Russia, according to the Larousse Gastronomique, *coulibiac was also prepared with chicken. If you think you'd prefer a chicken coulibiac, substitute cooked breast of chicken, cut into large pieces, for the fish in either of the two preceding coulibiac recipes and serve with a Béchamel Sauce (page 201) instead of the sauces indicated.*

CHAPTER SEVEN

PÂTÉS IN THE NEW CUISINE MANNER: SEAFOOD, VEGETABLE, AND TOFU

The Nouvelle Cuisine idea that started in France arrived on these shores and was welcomed, adopted, and changed to the New American Cuisine. What is the essence of our new cuisine? It's light and natural without sacrificing a hedonistic approach to the multi-flavored pleasures of the table. Quality of ingredients is high, and those ingredients are native grown.

The New American Cuisine emphasizes vegetables and seafood, and the result for pâté cookery is a lighter pâté, often lower in calories. Tofu—the healthy bean curd—is turned into a flavorful marvel when it becomes part of a pâté, and when it comes to a garnish, Golden Caviar from California is a favorite.

The New American Cuisine, like the Nouvelle Cuisine of France, offers both chef and guest a choice in the range of calories. The pâtés are often low in calories, while the sauces offered with them are high—but the sauces are on the side—and the tiniest dollop of rich sauce can make the difference between feeling deprived and feeling that one has eaten well.

CHICKEN SPINACH TERRINE

**2 chicken breasts, skinned and boned, cut into large
    cubes (about 2 pounds)**
1 pound chicken livers
2 tablespoons butter
1 medium onion, chopped
1 clove garlic, pressed
2 stalks celery, finely chopped
One 10-ounce package frozen chopped spinach, thawed
1 cup bread crumbs
2 eggs, beaten
¼ teaspoon celery salt
Salt and freshly ground black pepper to taste

Using a food processor, process chicken breasts until coarsely ground. Reserve.

Using a food processor, puree chicken livers. Reserve.

Heat butter in a medium skillet and sauté onion, garlic and celery for 3 minutes. Add chopped spinach to skillet and cook, stirring, for 5 minutes.

Spoon ingredients from skillet into a large bowl and add chicken, livers, and bread crumbs. Mix and add eggs and seasonings. Mix until all ingredients are thoroughly combined.

Spoon mixture into an 8-cup terrine and cover tightly with aluminum foil.

Place terrine in a bain-marie in a preheated 400° oven. Bake for 1½ hours. Cool before refrigerating. Chill for 4 to 6 hours before serving.

Serves 10 to 12.

VEGETABLE VEAL PÂTÉ

1 pound veal, cubed
1 egg
1½ cups crème fraîche (page 210)
¼ teaspoon coriander
Salt and freshly ground black pepper to taste
1 pound beets, cooked
1 pound carrots, cut into rounds, cooked for 10 minutes
Two 10-ounce packages frozen chopped spinach, cooked
Butter

Combine veal, egg, crème fraîche, and seasonings in a food processor and process until veal is ground and all ingredients are thoroughly combined. Reserve.

Using a food processor, chop beets finely. Reserve.

Repeat with carrots and with spinach, keeping each vegetable separate.

Divide ground veal mixture into thirds. Combine one-third of veal with beets, one-third with carrots, and one-third with spinach, keeping each mixture separate.

Butter an 8-cup terrine or a 9×5×3-inch loaf pan. Spoon the veal-beet mixture into the terrine. Smooth top and add veal-carrot mixture. Smooth top and add veal-spinach mixture.

Cover pan tightly with aluminum foil and place in a bain-marie in a preheated 350° oven. Bake for 1½ hours.

Remove foil and allow pâté to cool. Chill for 4 to 6 hours.

Serves 10 to 12.

SALMON PÂTÉ IN THE MANNER OF L'ESCOFFIER RESTAURANT

The L'Escoffier restaurant at the Beverly Hilton Hotel in Beverly Hills, California, follows in the traditional footsteps of the great master, Auguste Escoffier. Master Chef Raymond Dreyfus and the Director of the restaurant, Gilbert Paoli, diligently research and follow the ideas and recipes of Escoffier, and the following pâté is based on the famed Salmon Quenelles served at this elegant restaurant. The pâté is far easier to prepare than the quenelles; it is light, can be made in small amounts, and is wonderful when served at an important supper for two, with a perfectly chilled bottle of champagne.

> 1 pound fillet of salmon
> 1 teaspoon salt, or to taste
> ½ teaspoon freshly ground white pepper
> ¼ teaspoon nutmeg
> 2 egg whites
> 2 cups heavy sweet cream (whipping cream)
> Butter
> Lobster Sauce (page 197)

Cut salmon into large pieces and place in food processor. Add seasonings and grind fish coarsely.

With machine on, gradually add egg whites to fish. When egg whites have been incorporated into fish, gradually and slowly add heavy cream. Continue processing until cream has been thoroughly combined with salmon and mixture is a smooth puree.

Butter a 6-cup pâté mold or terrine. Spoon salmon forcemeat into mold and smooth top.

Cover pâté with foil and bake in a bain-marie in a preheated 350° oven for 30 minutes, or until pâté is firm.

Serve with Lobster Sauce.

Serves 2 to 4.

TRICOLOR TERRINE OF SCALLOPS FROM LES TROIS PETITS COCHONS

Since 1975 Les Trois Petits Cochons has been producing French pâtés that are sold around the country in fine food shops. Chef Jean-Pierre Pradie shares his recipe for one favorite: a 3-colored, 3-layered terrine of scallops.

The Chef says: "This terrine may be eaten cold with a mayonnaise-based sauce, or hot with a beurre à l'échalote sauce or a lobster sauce. When preparing the terrine make sure the ingredients are very, very cold!"

- **1½ pounds bay or sea scallops**
- **3 small cloves garlic**
- **3 small shallots**
- **Salt and freshly ground white pepper to taste**
- **Pinch of nutmeg**
- **3 tablespoons cognac**
- **Pinch of saffron**
- **3 eggs**
- **3 cups heavy sweet cream (whipping cream)**
- **1 large bunch parsley (about 3 cups, packed), blanched**
- **1 tablespoon tomato paste**
- **Butter**
- **Beurre à l'Échalote Sauce (page 196) *or***
- **Lobster Sauce (page 197)**

Divide scallops into three ½-pound portions and place each portion on foil. Add 1 clove garlic and 1 shallot to each portion. Season each portion with salt, pepper, and nutmeg. Wrap each portion in foil and place in freezer to chill.

Heat 1 tablespoon cognac, stir in saffron, pour into a small bowl and chill in refrigerator.

Remove 1 portion of scallops from freezer and, using a food processor, process with 1 egg and 1 tablespoon of cognac. Gradually add 1 cup cream and process until ingredients are pureed and thoroughly blended. Spoon into a bowl and refrigerate.

Remove second portion of scallops from freezer and, using a food processor, blend with blanched parsley and 1 egg and 1 tablespoon cognac. Gradually add 1 cup of cream and process until ingredients are pureed and thoroughly blended. Spoon into another bowl and refrigerate.

Remove last portion of scallops from freezer and, using a food processor, blend with tomato paste, 1 egg, and cognac-saffron mixture. Gradually add last cup of cream and process until ingredients are pureed and thoroughly blended. Spoon into another bowl and refrigerate.

Butter a 9×5×3-inch loaf pan or a 2-quart terrine. Spoon in the first portion of scallop puree and smooth top with a spatula. Spoon in scallop-parsley mixture and smooth top with a spatula. Top with scallop-tomato paste mixture and smooth over with a spatula. Cover terrine with foil and bake in a bain-marie in a preheated 250° oven for 2½ hours, or until a thin skewer comes out clean after piercing center of terrine.

Serve with Beurre à l'Échalote Sauce or with Lobster Sauce.

Serves 8 to 12.

SALMON PÂTÉ WITH SCALLOPS

1½ pounds salmon, cubed
1 egg
2 cups crème fraîche (page 210)
Salt and freshly ground white pepper to taste
2 tablespoons butter
2 green onions (scallions)
1 pound bay scallops
Butter
4 fillets of flounder, thinly cut (about 1 pound)
Sauce Verte (page 186)

Using a food processor, puree salmon, gradually adding egg, crème fraîche, and seasonings. Spoon salmon puree into a bowl and reserve.

Heat butter in a large skillet and add green onions and scallops. Cook, stirring, for 3 minutes. Stir contents of skillet into salmon mixture and combine.

Butter an 8-cup pâté mold or a 9×5×3-inch loaf pan. Cut each fillet of flounder in half lengthwise and place 2 pieces of flounder on the bottom of the mold. Top with a layer of salmon mixture and continue alternating layers, finishing with salmon mixture.

Smooth top layer and cover mold or pan tightly with aluminum foil. Place the mold in a bain-marie in a preheated 350° oven and bake for 1½ hours. Allow pâté to cool and refrigerate for 4 to 6 hours. Slice and serve with Sauce Verte.

Serves 8 to 12.

AVOCADO AND
SHRIMP PÂTÉ

4 ripe avocados
1 tablespoon unflavored gelatin (1 packet)
¼ cup water
1 shallot, minced
1 tablespoon brandy
¾ cup heavy sweet cream (whipping cream)
1 egg yolk
½ cup chicken broth
Salt and freshly ground white pepper to taste
Butter
½ pound cooked, chopped shrimp
Pimiento Sauce (page 187)

Peel and seed avocados and, using a food processor, chop coarsely. Sprinkle gelatin on ¼ cup water and let stand until softened. Combine avocados in processor with gelatin, shallot, brandy, cream, egg yolk, broth, and seasonings and process until just combined. Spoon half of mixture into a buttered 9×5×3-inch loaf pan. Top with shrimp. Spread remaining avocado mixture over shrimp.

Place loaf pan in a bain-marie and bake in a preheated 325° oven for 45 minutes. Decrease heat to 300° and bake 10 minutes longer.

Remove pâté from oven and cool. Refrigerate for 4 hours. Serve with Pimiento Sauce.

Serves 10.

SPINACH AND OYSTER PÂTÉ WITH FENNEL

6 tablespoons butter
3 shallots, minced
1 cup finely chopped fresh fennel (called finocchio at
    Italian vegetable shops); if fresh fennel is unavailable,
    use 2 teaspoons fennel seeds
Two 10-ounce packages frozen chopped spinach, thawed
1 cup heavy sweet cream (whipping cream)
6 slices white bread, torn into small pieces
3 eggs, beaten
Salt and freshly ground black pepper to taste
2 cups shelled oysters
Butter
Beurre Blanc Sauce I or II (page 183 or 184)

Heat the butter in a skillet and sauté the shallots and fennel for 3 minutes, stirring. Add spinach and continue cooking until spinach has wilted and water from spinach has evaporated.

Add cream and continue cooking for 3 minutes. Spoon contents of skillet into a food processor and add bread, eggs, seasonings, and oysters. Process until all ingredients are combined and oysters are coarsely chopped.

Butter a 9×5×3-inch loaf pan and spoon in spinach-oyster mixture. Smooth the top, cover with foil, and place pan in a bain-marie in a preheated 350° oven. Bake for 1 hour. Serve with Beurre Blanc Sauce.

Serves 6 to 8.

TERRINE OF SHRIMP

2 pounds shrimp, shelled and deveined
3 tablespoons butter
Salt to taste
¼ teaspoon hot pepper sauce or Tabasco
2 tablespoons Pernod or Sambuca liqueur
¼ teaspoon anise seeds
2½ cups heavy sweet cream (whipping cream)
Butter
Sauce Verte (page 186)

Depending on size of shrimp, reserve 5 to 7 shrimp for decorating top of terrine.

Heat butter in a large skillet. Season the 5 to 7 shrimp with salt and hot pepper sauce and sauté in butter for 3 to 5 minutes, or until shrimp turn pink. Remove from heat, add liqueur to pan, stir, and reserve.

Combine uncooked shrimp and anise seeds in a food processor. Add cream, gradually, and process until shrimp are pureed and cream is incorporated into mixture. Spoon pureed shrimp into a bowl. Remove shrimp from skillet and stir sauce from skillet into pureed shrimp mixture, mixing thoroughly.

Butter a 2-quart terrine or a 9×5×3-inch loaf pan. Spoon shrimp mixture into terrine and smooth top. Place cooked whole shrimp on top of terrine, pressing lightly into shrimp mixture.

Cover terrine tightly with foil and place in a bain-marie in a preheated 325° oven. Bake for 1¼ hours.

Allow terrine to cool and refrigerate for 4 to 6 hours. Serve with Sauce Verte.

Serves 8 to 10.

TERRINE OF FISH FILLETS WITH FRESH VEGETABLES

A low-calorie terrine from France! The land of cream, butter, and crème fraîche offers a delicious terrine made this time with low-fat yogurt and low-fat cottage cheese.

2 eggs, lightly beaten
1 small onion, minced
One 8-ounce container low-fat yogurt
One 8-ounce container low-fat cottage cheese
½ teaspoon coriander seed
¼ teaspoon anise seed
Freshly ground black pepper to taste
1 pound fillet of fish (may be flounder, sole, or cod), cut into thin slices
8 baby carrots, cut into narrow strips
1 pound broccoli, separated into small flowerets

Using a food processor, combine eggs, onion, yogurt, cottage cheese, and spices, mixing thoroughly.

Divide fish fillets in half. Place half the fillets, lengthwise, in a 6-cup terrine. Spoon egg-cheese mixture on top of fish and smooth to even out. Place vegetable pieces carefully on top of egg-cheese mixture. Top with remaining fish slices. Cover terrine with lid or with foil and bake in a preheated 350° oven for 45 minutes.

Serves 4 to 6.

TERRINE OF SALMON FROM THE LOIRE VALLEY

1½ pounds fillets of whiting or gray sole, cut into large
    pieces
2 egg whites
2 cups crème fraîche (page 210), chilled
Salt and freshly ground white pepper to taste
Butter
2 pounds salmon fillets, thinly sliced
Sauce Ciboulette (page 189)

Using a food processor, puree fillets of whiting or gray sole, gradually adding egg whites, crème fraîche, and seasonings. Process until all ingredients are thoroughly combined.

Butter a 2-quart pâté mold or a 9×5×3-inch loaf pan and spread a layer of pureed fish in the bottom. Cover with a layer of salmon slices and continue layering, finishing with a layer of pureed fish.

Place pâté mold in a bain-marie in a preheated 350° oven and cook for 1 hour, or until a thin skewer inserted in center comes out clean.

Allow pâté to cool, and refrigerate for 2 to 4 hours. Unmold, and serve with Sauce Ciboulette.

Serves 8.

TERRINE OF SEA URCHIN FROM LE GOURMET RESTAURANT

This terrine was created by a gifted chef, Roy Yamaguchi, for Le Gourmet, a restaurant that the Sheraton Plaza La Reina Hotel in Los Angeles is justly proud of. The menu is a combination of the Orient and France, and this terrine is a fine example of the blending of two great cuisines.

The recipe calls for sea urchin roe, which is readily available in California, but not so easily found in the rest of the country. The same is true for shiso leaves. We asked Chef Yamaguchi about substitutes.

"There is no substitute for shiso leaves," said Roy Yamaguchi. "It has a unique flavor. And while you could substitute crab meat for the urchin roe, it just wouldn't be the same."

Here then, is the recipe for Terrine of Sea Urchin—without substitutes. Roy Yamaguchi, who is just opening his own restaurant in Los Angeles—385, by name—recommends preparing this unique dish with the proper ingredients or preparing another terrine instead.

> ½ **pound bay or sea scallops**
> ¼ **pound fillet of snapper**
> ¼ **pound fillet of pike**
> ¼ **pound sea urchin roe**
> 1½ **cups heavy sweet cream (whipping cream)**
> ¼ **pound butter, softened**
> 3 **ounces fish stock**
> **Salt and freshly ground white pepper**
> 40 **leaves of shiso (Japanese beefsteak plant), cut into julienne strips**

Butter
1 pound sea urchin roe
Tomato Shiso Vinaigrette Sauce (page 194)
Chive Mustard Sauce (page 195)

Using a food processor, puree scallops, snapper, pike, and ¼ pound of sea urchin roe. Gradually add cream, ¼ pound butter, and fish stock and process until mixture is well combined. Season, spoon into a bowl, and chill for 2 hours.

Remove from refrigerator and stir in julienne strips of shiso. Butter a 2-quart terrine and alternate layers of fish puree with layers of sea urchin roe, finishing with puree.

Cover terrine with foil and bake in a bain-marie in a 350° oven for 1 hour, or until a thin skewer inserted in center of terrine comes out clean. Serve with both Tomato Shiso Vinaigrette Sauce and Chive Mustard Sauce.

Serves 8.

PÂTÉ OF SALMON EN CROÛTE

1½ pounds fillet of salmon
1 cup dry white wine
½ pound cooked chopped shrimp
½ pound mushrooms, coarsely chopped
½ cup heavy sweet cream (whipping cream)
Salt and freshly ground white pepper to taste
Pâte brisée I, doubled (page 22)
1 egg yolk, lightly beaten
Shrimp Butter (page 204)

Place salmon in a shallow dish, pour wine over fish, and marinate salmon, turning every 15 minutes, for 2 hours.

In a saucepan combine shrimp, mushrooms, and cream and cook over low heat, for 2 minutes. Season and reserve.

Roll out pastry to fit a deep-dish pie plate or casserole.

Drain salmon and cut into large pieces. Place salmon pieces in pie plate and top with shrimp-mushroom mixture. Cover with remaining pastry, carefully sealing edges. Cut a small hole in center of pastry and pierce pastry with a fork. Brush pastry with egg yolk and bake pâté in a 350° oven for 1 hour.

Slice and serve with a dollop of Shrimp Butter on each portion.

Serves 4 to 6.

PÂTÉ OF SMOKED FISH

The recipe was created by André Mercier, a fine French chef, who has, since coming to the United States, been head chef for a large hotel chain, owner of the Mirabeau Restaurant in Oakland, California, and is currently a food consultant.

This pâté is equally delicious whether it's made with smoked sturgeon or smoked salmon trout, products available under a number of brand names, among them Tsar Nicoulai—the same clever California company that brought Golden Caviar to a peak of popularity and prominence around the country.

> 1 tablespoon (1 packet) unflavored gelatin
> ½ cup cold water
> ½ cup dry white Burgundy
> 1 pound smoked fish (may be salmon trout or sturgeon), boned and skinned
> 2 tablespoons lemon juice
> Salt and freshly ground black pepper to taste
> Pinch of cayenne pepper
> 2 cups heavy sweet cream (whipping cream), whipped
> Butter
> Lemon-Chive Sabayon (page 182)

In the top of a double boiler, soften gelatin in water. Over low heat, cook gelatin mixture, stirring, until gelatin is dissolved. Add wine, stir, and remove from heat. Reserve.

Using a food processor, process fish until it is a smooth puree. Spoon into a bowl and stir in cooled gelatin mixture, lemon juice, salt, pepper, and cayenne. Fold whipped cream into fish puree, blending carefully.

Spoon fish mixture into a buttered 6-cup mold. Tap sides of mold with a knife handle to settle mixture and refrigerate until set—about 4 to 6 hours.

Serve with Lemon-Chive Sabayon.

Serves 6 to 8.

RILLETTES D'AUBERGINE

2 large, or 3 or 4 small, eggplants
Salt
3 cloves garlic
2 tablespoons yogurt
¼ cup olive oil
1 tablespoon lemon juice
Freshly ground black pepper to taste
Fresh or dried chopped mint leaves

Cut eggplants in half. Cut into flesh of eggplant, making several deep gashes. Sprinkle eggplant halves liberally with salt. Place eggplant halves, flesh side down, on several plates or 1 large platter for 45 minutes. The salt will draw some of the bitter liquid out of the eggplant. Rinse eggplant halves well and pat dry with paper towels.

Bake eggplant halves in a preheated 350° oven for 20 to 30 minutes, or until eggplants are tender and skin is charred. Allow eggplants to cool and then peel off skin.

Using a food processor, puree eggplants with garlic. Add yogurt, oil, lemon juice, and pepper. Process until thoroughly combined. Spoon into a 3- to 4-cup crock. Garnish with chopped mint and chill for 1 hour. Serve with pita bread.

Serves 6.

WILD RICE MEAT CAKE WITH CHEESE SAUCE

For Wild Rice Meat Cake:

1 pound beef, cubed
3 eggs, beaten
2 stalks celery, cut into 4 pieces
1 medium onion, quartered
¾ cup mushrooms
Salt and freshly ground black pepper to taste
2 cups cooked wild rice (about ½ cup uncooked)

For Cheese Sauce:

2 tablespoons butter
2 tablespoons all-purpose flour
1 cup milk
1 cup grated cheddar cheese, about ¼ pound
½ tablespoon Worcestershire sauce
⅛ teaspoon Tabasco or hot pepper sauce

Combine beef, eggs, celery, onion, mushrooms, salt and pepper in a food processor. Process until beef is coarsely ground and all other ingredients are chopped. Spoon into a bowl and stir in rice. Mix thoroughly.

Spoon meat mixture into a 9×5×3-inch loaf pan and bake in a preheated 350° oven for 1 hour.

To make cheese sauce:

Melt butter over low heat and stir in flour, blending well. Slowly stir in the milk, stirring constantly. Cook until smooth and thickened. Add cheese and seasonings and stir until cheese melts.

After meat cake is cooked, let cool at room temperature for 10 minutes. Drain excess juices from pan and turn meat cake out onto serving platter. Slice and spoon cheese sauce over all.

Serves 6.

SPINACH PÂTÉ IN PHYLLO DOUGH

¼ **pound butter**
Four 10-ounce packages frozen chopped spinach, thawed
4 shallots, finely chopped
3 eggs, lightly beaten
½ **cup creamed cottage cheese**
⅓ **cup crumbled blue or Roquefort cheese**
½ **cup boiled ham, cubed**
Salt and freshly ground black pepper to taste
14 sheets phyllo dough
¼ **pound butter, melted**

Heat ¼ pound butter in a large skillet or a saucepan and cook spinach, stirring, for 5 minutes, or until spinach liquid has evaporated. Add shallots to spinach, stir, and cook for an additional 3 to 5 minutes.

Using a food processor, puree spinach-shallot mixture with eggs until just combined. Add cottage cheese, blue or Roquefort cheese, ham, and seasonings. Process until all ingredients are thoroughly combined.

Lay out the sheets of phyllo dough between two damp dish cloths. Remove and brush 1 sheet with melted butter. Transfer it to a buttered 9×5×3-inch loaf pan. Butter another sheet of phyllo and transfer to loaf pan. Continue until 10 sheets of phyllo dough have been placed in loaf pan, with edges hanging over long sides of pan. Butter remaining 4 sheets of dough and place in pan so that dough hangs over ends of pan. Spoon spinach mixture into pan and bring up edges of phyllo dough to enclose the top completely. Brush with remaining melted butter and bake in a preheated 400° oven for 1 hour, or until pastry is golden brown.

Serves 6.

TRADER VIC'S TOFU CHICKEN LIVER PÂTÉ IN ASPIC

When Queen Elizabeth and Prince Phillip visited the United States they dined with Nancy Reagan at a gala dinner at San Francisco's Trader Vic's. Here—and probably for the first time—is the recipe for the Tofu Chicken Liver Pâté that was among the appetizers served at the festive event.

**6 tablespoons butter
1½ pounds chicken livers
1 tablespoon finely chopped shallots
½ teaspoon salt
¼ teaspoon mace
¼ teaspoon nutmeg
½ teaspoon sage
2 ounces brandy
2 ounces heavy sweet cream (whipping cream)
6 ounces tofu (bean curd)
2 ounces Havarti cheese
2 ounces cream cheese
7 tablespoons plain gelatin (7 packets)
12 ounces chicken or beef broth
2 hard-cooked eggs, chopped
¼ cup chopped pistachio nuts**

Heat butter in a skillet and sauté livers and shallots, stirring, for 3 minutes. Add seasonings and cook until liver is medium-rare. Add brandy and flame, tossing until flames die out. Spoon liver and sauce from skillet into a food processor and add cream, tofu, Havarti cheese, and cream cheese.

Combine gelatin and 4 ounces broth and mix into a thick paste. Add half of gelatin paste to liver mixture, reserving other half. Process liver-gelatin mixture until all ingredients are well combined and smooth. Reserve.

To make aspic: Combine remaining gelatin paste with 8 ounces broth. Heat to dissolve gelatin and spoon half aspic mixture into the bottom of a 1-quart loaf pan. Chill. Top with the chopped eggs and chill until firm.

Spoon liver mixture on top of aspic and chill until firm.

Spoon remaining aspic on top of liver mixture. Garnish with pistachio nuts and chill until firm.

Slice thinly and serve with buttered rye bread that has also been cut into thin slices.

Serves 12 to 15.

TRADER VIC'S DINNER FOR QUEEN ELIZABETH, PRINCE PHILIP, AND FIRST LADY NANCY REAGAN

The following dinner, arranged by Mr. Bill Chow of Trader Vic's in San Francisco, was served to the Queen of England, Prince Philip, First Lady Nancy Reagan, and 52 honored guests.

Queen's Menu:

Before Dinner: Almadén Blanc de Blancs Champagne
Hanzell Chardonnay

Appetizers: Peach Blossom Duck Tidbits
Sliced Barbecued Pork
Cho Cho
Smoked Salmon Canapés
Tofu Chicken Liver Pâté Canapés
Szechwan Cheese Wonton
Langostinos Opu

Wine: Stonehill Chardonnay 1980

Salad: Agar-Agar Limestone Lettuce with Wasabi
Dressing

Wine: Stonehill Chardonnay 1980

Entrée: Indonesian Lamb Roast
Peanut Sauce
Peach Chutney

	Asparagus Chinese Style
	Pake Noodles
Wine:	Beaulieu (P.R.) 1971
Dessert:	Rum Ice Cream with Praline Sauce
	Cookies
Wine:	Almadén Blanc de Blancs
	Coffee
	Tea
	Mints

TRADER VIC'S
TOFU VEAL PÂTÉ

6 tablespoons butter
1½ pounds veal, diced
½ pound tofu (bean curd)
1 teaspoon salt
½ teaspoon mace
½ teaspoon sage
½ teaspoon nutmeg
1 tablespoon seasoning salt
½ teaspoon black pepper
4 ounces brandy
6 ounces Havarti cheese
**5 tablespoons unflavored gelatin (5 packets), combined
    with 4 ounces chicken or beef broth**
1 cup heavy sweet cream (whipping cream)
½ cup chopped pistachio nuts

Heat butter in a skillet and sauté veal for 3 minutes. Allow to cool. Place all remaining ingredients, except cream and pistachio nuts, in a food processor and grind very fine. Spoon mixture into a bowl and fold in heavy cream and pistachio nuts.

Spoon mixture into a 1-quart loaf pan.

Place pan in a bain-marie and bake in a preheated 375° oven for 45 minutes.

Cool pâté. Refrigerate for 4 to 6 hours, or until thoroughly chilled.

Slice thinly and serve.

Serves 12 to 15.

PÂTÉ POSTSCRIPT FROM TRADER VIC'S:

Mr. Bill Chow of Trader Vic's says emphatically, "Do not freeze tofu pâtés!"

TOFU TERRINE KAHALA

The best hotel in Honolulu is light-years in spirit away from the noisy center of Waikiki. It's located in the Kahala section and is part of the Hilton International chain. The Kahala Hilton has dreamlike views, frolicking dolphins, concerned service, and excellent restaurants with an international point of view. One fine example of their cuisine is their Tofu Terrine, based on a recipe from Hilton International files.

>   1 pound tofu (bean curd)
>   3 eggs
>   ½ cup cooked spinach puree
>   ½ cup cooked carrot puree
>   1 teaspoon sesame oil
>   Salt and freshly ground white pepper to taste
>   4 ounces tofu (bean curd)
>   1 tablespoon cooked asparagus puree
>   Tomato Concasse (page 188)

Using a food processor, puree 1 pound tofu and eggs until smooth. Divide tofu puree into 3 equal parts, and reserve 1 part.

Combine one part tofu puree with spinach puree and mix thoroughly. Reserve.

Combine another part of tofu puree with carrot puree and mix thoroughly. Reserve.

Line a 2-quart pâté mold or a 9×5×3-inch loaf pan with cheesecloth. Season the reserved plain tofu mixture with sesame oil, salt and pepper, and mix well, spreading this plain tofu in bottom of the mold. Smooth top. Carefully spoon tofu-spinach mixture into pan, smoothing top. Cover with tofu-carrot mixture and smooth top. Draw ends of cheesecloth over pâté to cover and bake in a bain-marie in a preheated 350° oven for 10 to 15 minutes, or until a sharp knife inserted in center of pâté comes out dry.

Allow terrine to cool completely before slicing.

Combine 4 ounces tofu with asparagus puree in a food processor. Process until completely mixed and smooth.

Spoon asparagus mixture onto a serving platter. Place terrine slices in center and serve with Tomato Concasse.

Serves 8 to 10.

LAYERED TOFU
TERRINE FROM JAPAN

2 pounds tofu (bean curd)
1 tablespoon all-purpose flour
1 egg white
1 carrot, sliced
1 pound beef, cubed
2 eggs
1 small onion, quartered
2 slices bread, torn into large pieces
2 tablespoons soy sauce
2 tablespoons duck sauce
Salt and freshly ground black pepper to taste
1 tablespoon vegetable oil
1½ tablespoons all-purpose flour

Combine tofu, flour, egg white, and carrot in a food processor and process until thoroughly combined. Spoon into a bowl and reserve.

Combine beef with eggs, onion, bread, soy sauce, duck sauce, salt and pepper in a food processor. Process until beef is ground and all ingredients are thoroughly combined.

Coat a 9×5×3-inch loaf pan with oil and dust with ½ tablespoon flour; shake out excess flour. Spoon half the meat mixture into pan, spreading evenly. Top with all of the tofu mixture, spreading evenly. Sprinkle on 1 tablespoon flour and top with remaining meat mixture.

Bake in a preheated 350° oven for 40 minutes.

Serves 6 to 8.

CHAPTER EIGHT

ELEGANT AND INEXPENSIVE

Pâtés offer the best of both worlds: they can be elegant and inexpensive at the same time, attributes not found together in too many other areas of cuisine. The elegant-inexpensive combination does not include the game pâtés, or the salmon and sole pâtés—not since fish has become more expensive than steak. But it does include rustic pâtés, Italian tortas, sausage pâtés enclosed in a flaky pastry crust, pâtés de campagne, and some American meat and fish pies.

Elegant and inexpensive pâtés are imaginative: wild rice is used in small amounts, and gâteaux and pains de viandes rely on the small touches—grated coconut, for example, or a flavoring of wine. The pâtés in this chapter are bound to become favorites because the richness of flavor can be enjoyed no matter the state of your exchequer.

ROAST GOOSE PÂTÉ

2 tablespoons goose fat (use drippings from roasting goose)
1 pound chicken livers, cut in half
Salt and freshly ground black pepper to taste
1 tablespoon unflavored gelatin (1 packet)
1¼ cups chicken broth
1 cup chopped leftover roast goose
1 medium onion, quartered
½ cup heavy sweet cream (whipping cream)
½ cup mayonnaise
¼ teaspoon Worcestershire sauce
Salt and freshly ground black pepper to taste

Heat fat in skillet, add livers, salt, and pepper and sauté until lightly browned. Reserve.

Sprinkle gelatin over ¼ cup cold broth in food processor bowl. Heat remaining 1 cup broth and pour over softened gelatin. Add goose, onion, chicken livers, cream, mayonnaise, Worcestershire sauce, salt and pepper. Process until smooth.

Spoon into a lightly oiled 1-quart pâté mold or crock. Chill for 4 to 6 hours. Unmold onto a serving platter, or serve from crock. Serve with pumpernickel bread or crackers.

Serves 6 to 8.

SMOKED TURKEY PÂTÉ WITH WALNUTS

2 cups toasted walnuts
4 cups cooked turkey, cut into large pieces
4 tablespoons butter, softened
1 small onion, quartered
¼ teaspoon hickory liquid smoke
1 teaspoon hickory smoked salt
½ cup mayonnaise

Combine 1½ cups of the walnuts with turkey, butter, onion, liquid smoke, smoked salt, and mayonnaise in a food processor and process until turkey is finely ground and all ingredients are thoroughly combined. Spoon into a 4-cup crock, cover, and refrigerate for 2–4 hours to blend flavors.

Before serving, chop remaining ½ cup toasted walnuts in food processor and sprinkle over pâté.

Serves 6 to 8.

EASY CHICKEN LIVER PÂTÉ IN PASTRY CRUST

1 pound chicken livers, cut in half
2 eggs
1 tablespoon brandy
¾ cup heavy sweet cream (whipping cream)
1 small onion, quartered
¼ cup all-purpose flour
½ teaspoon ground cardamom
Salt and freshly ground white pepper to taste
½ teaspoon ground cumin
Butter
Pâte brisée I, doubled (page 22)
1 egg, beaten

Using a food processor, combine livers with eggs, brandy, cream, onion, flour, and seasonings and process until mixture is smooth and thoroughly blended.

Butter a 16×3×3-inch pan.

Roll out pâte brisée and line pan with the pastry, allowing it to hang over ends and sides of pan. Spoon liver pâté into pan and fold pastry over pâté, sealing edges carefully.

Make rosettes out of pastry scraps and decorate center of the pâté, covering the seam. Pierce each rosette with a sharp knife and prick pastry with a fork around the edges of the pâté.

Brush pastry with beaten egg and bake in a preheated 350° oven for approximately 45 minutes, or until pastry is brown.

Serves 8.

PÂTÉ DUBONNET

1 pound boiled ham, cubed
1 pound pork, cubed
1 pound veal, cubed
8 juniper berries
2 cloves garlic
½ teaspoon thyme
½ teaspoon nutmeg
⅔ cup Dubonnet Blanc
8 slices bacon
Orange-Lemon Sauce (page 185)

Combine ham, pork, veal, juniper berries, garlic, thyme, and nutmeg in a food processor. Grind coarsely and spoon into a bowl. Pour Dubonnet Blanc over all and marinate for 1 hour.

Using a food processor, process marinated meat mixture until finely ground and thoroughly combined.

Line bottom of a 6-cup terrine or loaf pan with 4 bacon strips. Spoon in meat mixture and smooth top. Cover with remaining bacon strips. Bake terrine in a bain-marie in a preheated 300° oven for 2½ hours, or until pâté is firm and has shrunk from the sides of the terrine.

Cool and refrigerate. Remove bacon strips. Slice pâté thinly and serve with Orange-Lemon Sauce.

Serves 12 to 15.

PÂTÉ FROM LEFTOVERS

4 tablespoons butter
1 large onion, finely chopped
2 cloves garlic, minced
3 cups leftover roast beef, lamb, or pork
1 large potato, cooked and mashed
¼ pound pork sausage meat
3 eggs, beaten
½ cup grated Gruyère cheese
⅛ teaspoon ground thyme
¼ teaspoon ground basil
Salt and freshly ground black pepper to taste

Heat butter in a skillet and sauté onion and garlic for 3 to 5 minutes, or until onion is translucent.

Using a food processor, coarsely grind leftover meat.

Combine butter-onion-garlic mixture with ground meat in food processor. Add other ingredients one at a time, processing until all ingredients are thoroughly combined.

Spoon mixture into a 6-cup loaf pan or pâté mold. Bake in a preheated 350° oven for 1 hour. Serve hot.

Serves 4.

SOUTHERN SAUSAGE CAKE WITH CORNMEAL LATTICE

½ cup all-purpose flour
2 tablespoons cornmeal
⅛ teaspoon salt
3 tablespoons lard
2–3 tablespoons cold water
2 pounds pork sausage meat
1 large pear, coarsely grated
¾ cup quick or old-fashioned oatmeal, uncooked
2 tablespoons catsup
1 small onion, quartered
1 tablespoon prepared horseradish
1 teaspoon Dijon mustard
2 eggs, beaten
2 teaspoons water

To make pastry: Combine flour, cornmeal, and salt in a food processor. Add lard and process until mixture resembles coarse crumbs. Add cold water, 1 tablespoon at a time, until mixture forms ball. Refrigerate pastry while you prepare sausage cake.

Combine pork sausage meat, pear, oatmeal, catsup, onion, horseradish, and mustard in a food processor. Reserve 1 tablespoon beaten egg and add remainder to sausage mixture. Process until all ingredients are thoroughly combined. Form meat mixture into jelly-roll shape, approximately 8 inches long and 4 inches wide, wrap in foil and refrigerate while preparing cornmeal pastry lattice strips.

Roll out pastry on a lightly floured board into a rectangle 8× 10 inches. Cut pastry into 8 strips, each about ¾ inch wide and about 7 inches long.

Place sausage cake in a shallow baking pan and place pastry strips over cake, crosswise, to cover top and sides. Try to space strips evenly. Combine reserved tablespoon of beaten egg with 2 teaspoons water, mix well, and brush pastry with this egg-water mixture.

Bake sausage cake in a preheated 375° oven for 1 hour.

Serves 8.

TEX-MEX MEAT PIE

1½ pounds beef, cubed
1 small onion, quartered
1 small green pepper, quartered
1 tablespoon vegetable oil
1 can (16 ounces) chili with beans
1 cup sifted all-purpose flour
½ teaspoon salt, or to taste
½ cup cornmeal
4–6 tablespoons lard
2–4 tablespoons cold water
½ cup shredded cheddar cheese

Combine beef, onion and green pepper in a food processor and grind coarsely.

Heat oil in a large skillet and sauté beef, onion, and green pepper, stirring, until ground beef is lightly browned. Pour off drippings. Add chili to ground beef mixture and mix well. Reserve.

To make pastry: Combine flour, salt, and cornmeal in a food processor. Add lard and process until mixture resembles coarse crumbs. Add water, 1 tablespoon at a time, until mixture forms a ball.

Roll out pastry on a lightly floured board to ⅛-inch thickness. Line a 9-inch pie pan with pastry. Spoon ground beef-chili mixture into pastry-lined pie pan. Bake in a preheated 425° oven for 15 minutes. Sprinkle with shredded cheese and continue baking an additional 5 minutes.

Serves 6.

ZURICH MEAT PIE

Another great way to use leftover roast meat, this recipe comes from the frugal and practical Swiss. You may use roast pork, veal, or beef—or any combination of the meats, should you have more than one kind of roast left over from a large party.

> 2–3 cups roast pork, veal, or beef, cut into large pieces
> ½ cup grapes or raisins
> 2 slices bacon, finely diced
> ¼ cup heavy sweet cream (whipping cream)
> 1 egg, lightly beaten
> Salt and freshly ground black pepper to taste
> Pinch of powdered cloves, or to taste
> Pinch of sugar, or to taste
> Pâte brisée I, doubled (page 22)
> 2 tablespoons butter
> 1 egg yolk, beaten with 1 tablespoon water

In a food processor, combine all ingredients except pastry, butter, and egg yolk. Process until meat is coarsely ground and all ingredients are thoroughly combined. Reserve.

Roll out half of pâte brisée to approximately ½-inch thickness and line a 9-inch pie plate.

Spoon meat mixture into pie plate and dot with butter.

Roll out remainder of pastry and place on top of meat mixture. Press edges of pastry firmly together to seal and cut a small hole in center of pastry. Prick pastry with a fork and decorate top of pie with scraps of pastry.

Brush pastry with egg yolk mixture and bake in a preheated 400° oven for 45 minutes.

Serves 3 to 4.

PÂTÉ DE CAMPAGNE FROM CHAMBORD

½ **pound pork, cubed**
½ **pound fresh pork fat, cubed**
½ **pound breast of boned, skinned chicken, cubed**
Salt and freshly ground black pepper to taste
½ **teaspoon Herbes de Provence**
2 cloves garlic
1 small onion, quartered
4 tablespoons brandy
2 eggs
½ **pound pork liver, cut into large chunks**
Sheets of fresh pork fat or fatback, about ⅛ **inch thick,**
 to line terrine

Using a food processor, grind pork, ½ pound pork fat, chicken, seasonings, garlic, and onion until meat is finely ground. Add brandy and eggs and mix until all ingredients are thoroughly combined. Spoon into a large bowl and reserve.

Using a food processor, process pork liver until coarsely chopped and stir into meat mixture.

Line bottom and sides of an 8-cup terrine or loaf pan with sheets of pork fat or fatback and spoon meat mixture into terrine. Cover meat with another sheet of pork fat. Make sure that the fat is tucked in on sides and at the ends so mixture is completely covered. Seal the entire pan with foil. Set terrine in a bain-marie and bake in a preheated 350° oven for approximately 2 hours. Pâté is cooked when meat shrinks from sides of terrine or loaf pan in which it is cooking. Test for doneness by pressing top of pâté with a spoon. There should be no traces of pink in juices. Or you can test by piercing the center with a thin skewer. Skewer should come out clean.

Remove pâté from oven. Weight and cool. Refrigerate, with weights still on. Be sure not to pour off any of the cooking juices.

Chill pâté for 8 to 12 hours. You may serve right from the terrine.

Serves 12 to 14.

FARMER'S LIVER PÂTÉ

¾ **pound pork liver**
1 onion, quartered
1 clove garlic
2 cups chicken broth
3 green onions (scallions), cut in half
4 tablespoons butter
2 tablespoons mayonnaise
2 tablespoons brandy
1½ teaspoons Dijon mustard
½ teaspoon celery salt
Salt and freshly ground black pepper to taste
⅛ teaspoon ground thyme
Vegetable oil
1 small orange, thinly sliced

Combine pork liver, onion, garlic, and chicken broth in a saucepan. Bring to a boil. Reduce heat; cover and simmer for 20 to 30 minutes, or until liver is done. Drain, discarding all but pork liver.

Using a food processor, process liver with green onions and butter. Add mayonnaise, brandy, mustard, and seasonings and process until all ingredients are thoroughly blended and smooth.

Oil a 2-cup pâté mold or terrine. Spoon liver mixture into mold. Cover tightly with aluminum foil. Refrigerate 6 to 8 hours. Turn pâté out of mold or serve from terrine. Garnish with orange slices.

Serves 4 to 6.

GÂTEAU AMÉRICAIN
EN CROÛTE

There are a number of American-type restaurants in Paris, many of them clustered around the super-modern museum, the Pompidou, known in Paris as the Beaubourg, because of its location in the Beaubourg section of Paris. Some of the restaurants serve chili, others offer hamburgers, often avec fromage—*a cheeseburger—while one offers a Gâteau Américain en croûte, an individual meat cake, or meat pâté, wrapped in crust. What makes it American? The use of a barbecue sauce with which the meat is basted as it bakes.*

1 pound beef, cubed
½ pound pork, cubed
½ pound liver pâté or liver spread (may be canned)
4 slices bread, crusts removed, torn into large pieces
½ cup dry red wine
1 small onion, quartered
2 stalks celery, cut into large pieces
2 cloves garlic
Salt and freshly ground black pepper to taste
Butter
1 cup catsup
2 tablespoons Worcestershire sauce
2 tablespoons wine vinegar
1 teaspoon Dijon mustard
2 tablespoons brown sugar
⅓ teaspoon hot pepper sauce or Tabasco
Pâte brisée I (page 22)
Butter

In a food processor, combine beef, pork, liver pâté or liver spread, bread, wine, onion, celery, garlic, salt and pepper. Process until all ingredients are finely ground and well combined. Shape meat into 4 round cakes.

Butter a shallow baking pan. Place meat cakes in pan. Reserve.

Combine all remaining ingredients, except pâte brisée, and mix thoroughly. Brush or spoon half the sauce mixture over the meat and bake in a preheated 375° oven for 15 minutes. Spoon remainder of sauce over meat and bake an additional 20 minutes. Remove meat from oven and cool until meat can be easily handled—about 20 minutes.

Prepare pâte brisée and wrap each meat cake in pastry. Pierce top of pastry with a fork and place meat cakes on a buttered baking pan, seam side down.

Bake in a preheated 425° oven for 15 to 30 minutes, or until crust is brown. Serve hot or cold.

Serves 4.

PAIN DE JAMBON

2 tablespoons butter
1 small onion, finely chopped
2 tablespoons diced green pepper
2 cups boiled or baked ham, cubed
1 egg, lightly beaten
¼ teaspoon hot pepper sauce or Tabasco
2 large baking potatoes, baked
½ cup milk
½ cup sour cream
1 tablespoon fresh dill or parsley, minced
Salt and freshly ground white pepper to taste
Butter
½ cup bread crumbs
1 tablespoon butter

Heat 2 tablespoons butter in a skillet and sauté onion and green pepper until translucent. Allow to cool. Finely chop ham in a food processor and combine with ingredients in skillet. Add egg and hot pepper sauce. Mix thoroughly and reserve.

Scoop out baked potato pulp from potato shells into a saucepan. Add milk, sour cream, dill or parsley, and salt and pepper. Mash over low heat until all ingredients are thoroughly combined.

Butter a 2-quart pâté mold, terrine, or a 9×5×3-inch loaf pan. Spoon half the ham mixture into mold. Top with all of the potato mixture and finish with a layer of remaining ham mixture. Sprinkle bread crumbs on top, dot with 1 tablespoon butter.

Bake in a preheated 350° oven for 30 minutes, or until Pain de Jambon is hot and crusty brown on top.

Serves 4.

ITALIAN TORTA OF SPINACH AND RICOTTA CHEESE

One 10-ounce package frozen chopped spinach, thawed
2 tablespoons butter
⅛ teaspoon nutmeg
4 tablespoons grated Romano cheese
1 pound fresh ricotta cheese
½ cup crumbled gorgonzola cheese
1 egg, lightly beaten
¼ teaspoon thyme
¼ teaspoon basil
Salt and freshly ground black pepper to taste
Pâte brisée I, doubled (page 22)
1 medium onion, thinly sliced
1 tablespoon butter, melted

Sauté spinach in 2 tablespoons butter for approximately 3 minutes, or until liquid has evaporated. Season with nutmeg and allow spinach to cool for 5 minutes.

In a food processor, combine spinach with Romano cheese, ricotta, gorgonzola, egg, thyme, basil, salt, and pepper. Process until all ingredients are thoroughly combined.

Roll out pastry to fit a 9-inch pie pan. Spoon spinach mixture onto pastry and top with onion slices. Roll out pastry for top crust, cover pie, and seal edges. Cut a small hole in center of pastry and prick pastry with a fork. Brush with melted butter.

Bake torta in a preheated 400° oven for about 30 minutes, or until crust is brown.

Serves 4 to 6.

COCONUT BEEF GÂTEAU

This touch of exotica comes from the Bali Room, the best restaurant at the Hilton Hawaiian Village in Honolulu. Alfred Mueller, the Executive Chef at the hotel, is Swiss, and worked and studied in Amsterdam where he became interested in Indonesian cooking—The Indonesian rijsttafel is a great favorite in Holland.

Chef Mueller decided to develop an Indonesian menu for the Bali Room, and he takes pride in using such authentic ingredients as lemon grass, tamarind, Indonesian bay leaf, Indonesian sugar, and tiger prawns from Thailand. The Cold Peanut Sauce is made with American peanut butter, however, because "it's the best," according to Chef Mueller, "and it's used even in Indonesia."

Rempah, or Coconut Beef Fritters, is one of the fifteen courses served at the Bali Room's rijsttafel dinner. It has been adapted here into a beef gâteau—or beef cake—another example of the international quality of the pâté.

> 2 pounds beef, cubed
> 2 eggs
> 1 cup grated fresh coconut or dried coconut flakes, unsweetened
> 2 teaspoons chopped fresh coriander, *or* ½ teaspoon dried coriander
> 2 cloves garlic
> ¼ teaspoon cardamom
> ⅛ teaspoon hot chili pepper, or to taste
> Salt to taste
> Nasi Putih (page 213)
> Cold Peanut Sauce (page 200)

Combine beef and eggs in a food processor and process until meat is coarsely ground. Add grated fresh coconut or dried co-

---

conut flakes. (If you are only able to obtain sweetened grated coconut, soak coconut overnight, drain, press out excess liquid, and then add to beef.)

Add all other ingredients, except for Nasi Putih and Cold Peanut Sauce, and process until all ingredients are thoroughly combined.

Spoon meat mixture into a buttered 9-inch pie pan and bake in a 400° oven for 40 minutes. Serve with Nasi Putih and Cold Peanut Sauce.

Serves 4 to 6.

PÂTÉ DE CAMPAGNE FROM ARLES

1 pound veal, cubed
1 pound fat pork, cubed
½ pound pork liver, cubed
2 cloves garlic
½ pound fatback, finely diced
6 juniper berries, crushed
Salt and freshly ground black pepper to taste
¼ teaspoon quatre-épices (page 211)
¼ cup white vermouth
¼ cup brandy
Sheets of pork fat to line and cover pâté

Combine veal, fat pork, pork liver, and garlic in a food processor and grind. Spoon into a large bowl and add all other ingredients, except for sheets of pork fat. Cover and refrigerate for 4 hours.

Line a 3-quart terrine with sheets of fat. Fill terrine with meat mixture and cover completely with sheets of fat. Bake in a bain-marie in a preheated 325° oven for 2½ hours. Allow pâté to cool. Weight and refrigerate overnight.

Serves 15 to 18.

GÂTEAU DE JAMBON FROM MARTINIQUE

1 pound smoked cooked ham, cubed
1 pound pork shoulder, cubed
2 eggs
½ cup light cream
¾ cup bread crumbs
Salt and freshly ground black pepper to taste
¼ teaspoon allspice
Butter

SPICY GLAZE

1 cup dark brown sugar
3 teaspoons dry mustard
⅓ cup raspberry or blueberry vinegar
½ cup orange juice
1 tablespoon butter

Using a food processor, coarsely grind ham and pork shoulder with eggs. Gradually add cream, bread crumbs, and seasonings, processing until all ingredients are thoroughly mixed.

Butter a 3-quart round terrine and spoon meat mixture into terrine, smoothing top. Bake in a preheated 350° oven for 40 minutes.

Combine all ingredients for glaze in a saucepan. Stir to combine and cook over low heat for 10 minutes. Turn heat to medium and continue cooking for an additional 5 minutes; sugar should be dissolved and all ingredients blended.

Continue baking Gâteau de Jambon for another 40 minutes, basting with Spicy Glaze every 10 minutes.

Serves 8.

GÂTEAU DE VIANDES AVEC FROMAGE

1 pound beef, cubed
½ pound veal, cubed
½ pound lean pork, cubed
2 eggs
2 ounces instant oatmeal
½ green pepper, sliced
1 small onion, quartered
½ cup dry vermouth
Salt and freshly ground black pepper to taste
Butter
¼ cup sesame seeds
1 cup grated Swiss cheese

Place meats in a food processor and grind. Add eggs, oatmeal, green pepper, onion, vermouth, and salt and pepper and process until thoroughly combined.

Butter a shallow baking pan and spoon meat into pan. Form meat into a round cake—similar to a round loaf of bread. Using a knife, make 2 shallow cuts across the top of the meat. Bake in a preheated 350° oven for 50 minutes.

Remove meat from oven and sprinkle sesame seeds into grooves created when meat was slashed prior to cooking. Sprinkle cheese over top of meat and return to oven. Bake for an additional 10 to 20 minutes, or until cheese melts on top of meat.

Serves 6 to 8.

TOURTE DE VEAU AVEC CHAMPIGNONS

This elegant veal pie is made with leftover roast veal gussied up with mushrooms and baked in a crust. It's a wonderful answer to yesterday's roast breast of veal or shoulder of veal that seemed to loom so large in the refrigerator.

Leftover roast veal (enough to make 3 cups ground)
4 slices white bread
½ cup light sweet cream
2 tablespoons butter
1 small onion, finely chopped
2 tablespoons chopped chives
Salt and freshly ground black pepper to taste
½ cup veal gravy or beef broth
4 tablespoons butter
½ pound thinly sliced mushrooms
1 tablespoon chopped parsley
Butter
Pâte brisée I, doubled (page 22)
1 egg yolk, beaten

Place veal in a food processor.

Trim crusts from white bread and break bread into pieces. Add bread and cream to veal and process until combined.

Heat 2 tablespoons butter in a skillet and sauté onion for 3 minutes. Add chives and cook for an additional minute. Add contents of skillet, salt, pepper, and veal gravy or beef broth to meat mixture and process until combined. Remove to a bowl. Reserve.

Heat 4 tablespoons butter in a skillet and sauté mushrooms just until mushrooms release their liquid. Add parsley to mushrooms and stir into meat mixture.

Butter a tourtière, deep-dish pie pan or casserole and line with pâte brisée. Partially bake in a 450° oven for 8 minutes. Allow to cool for 10 minutes.

Mix meat-mushroom mixture thoroughly and spoon into partially baked pastry shell. Cover with top crust, sealing edges carefully, and cut a small hole in center. Brush pastry with beaten egg.

Bake in a preheated 375° oven for 40 to 45 minutes, or until crust is brown.

Serves 4 to 6.

FLOUNDER PIE

You could call it a Coulibiac of Flounder—after all, a coulibiac is a Russian fish pie—or you could call it a Tourte of Flounder; tourte is the word the French use for dishes of this kind. However, to call it a coulibiac or a tourte would be to deny its very American origin, and therefore this easy and delicious dish remains Flounder Pie.

> 1½ pounds fillet of flounder
> ¼ pound salt pork, finely diced
> 1 large onion, thinly sliced
> 2 large baking potatoes, diced and parboiled
> Butter
> Pâte brisée I, doubled (page 22)
> 1 cup milk
> 1 cup light sweet cream
> Salt and freshly ground white pepper to taste

Cut fish fillets into large pieces. Reserve.

Sauté salt pork in a skillet until fat renders and pieces of salt pork begin to brown. Add onion slices and cook, stirring, until onion slices become translucent. Add parboiled potatoes to skillet and cook for another minute, stirring until all ingredients are thoroughly combined.

Butter a deep-dish pie pan and line with pâte brisée. Place fish pieces on pastry and top with all ingredients from skillet.

Heat milk and cream together in a saucepan and, when liquid begins to simmer, pour over mixture in pie shell. Season and cover with a top crust, sealing edges carefully. Cut a small hole in center of crust and prick crust with a fork.

Bake in a preheated 350° oven for 35 to 45 minutes, or until crust is brown.

Serves 4 to 5.

TUNA AND WILD RICE TERRINE

    1 (6- to 7-ounce) can tuna in olive oil
    2 stalks celery, sliced
    1 small green pepper, chopped
    1 medium onion, chopped
    4 cups cooked wild rice (about 1 cup uncooked)
    ¼ cup chopped parsley
    3 eggs, beaten lightly
    Salt and freshly ground black pepper to taste
    Butter

Drain oil from tuna into small skillet and sauté the celery, green pepper, and onion for 3 minutes.

Combine the tuna with the rice, sautéed vegetables, parsley, eggs, salt and pepper.

Spoon into a lightly buttered 6-cup terrine or a 9×5×3-inch loaf pan and bake in a preheated 350° oven for 45 minutes. Let set at room temperature for 10 minutes.

Serves 4 to 6.

PÂTÉ POSTSCRIPT:

Turn yesterday's meat loaf into tonight's pâté by cutting meat loaf into cubes and spreading two sides with softened butter, two sides with Dijon mustard. Roll pâté cubes in chopped parsley and serve.

RILLETTES OF BEEF LIVER

2 tablespoons butter
1 pound sliced beef liver, cut into 1-inch strips
½ cup chopped onion
¼ cup dry sherry
1 package (3 ounces) cream cheese
2 hard-cooked eggs
Salt and freshly ground black pepper to taste
½ teaspoon dry mustard

Heat butter in a skillet and brown liver and onion, stirring frequently. Reduce heat and add sherry. Cover tightly and cook slowly for 5 minutes. Allow liver mixture to cool.

Place liver mixture in a food processor and puree until smooth.

Cut cream cheese into thirds and eggs into quarters and add to liver mixture. Add seasonings and process until thoroughly combined. Spoon into a 3-cup crock and chill overnight.

Serves 6 to 8.

RILLETTES DE DINDON

Leftover turkey was once a bore—"One day of turkey, ten days of hash," ran the old song. But now, this wonderful, economical bird can be used in far more interesting ways. A rillettes of turkey is one fine example, but just for fun, call it Rillettes de Dindon—because so many things do sound better in French.

> **2 cups chopped, roast turkey**
> **¼ pound butter, softened**
> **⅛ teaspoon Tabasco or hot pepper sauce**
> **Salt and freshly ground black pepper to taste**
> **2 tablespoons brandy (optional)**
> **10–15 blanched almonds**

Place turkey, butter, Tabasco or hot pepper sauce, seasonings, and brandy (if you wish), in food processor. Process until almost smooth. Add almonds and continue processing for about 1 minute. (Almonds should not be pureed, just chopped to give an interesting texture to the pâté.)

Spoon pâté into a 3-cup crock and chill for 2 to 4 hours. Serve with pita bread or Armenian lavash bread.

Serves 6.

RILLETTES OF EGGS MAHARAJAH

6 hard-cooked eggs
¼ cup toasted chopped almonds
½ cup mayonnaise
½ teaspoon curry powder
2 tablespoons chutney
Freshly ground white pepper to taste

Combine all ingredients in a food processor and process until all ingredients are combined and eggs are finely chopped. Do not overprocess. Spoon into a 2-cup crock and chill before serving. Serve with pappadums—Indian curry biscuits—or with crackers.

Serves 4 to 6.

RILLETTES DE THON

In France this rillettes is made with fresh poached tuna. However, it can also be prepared successfully with tuna that's been canned in water and is a fine change from too-familiar tuna salad.

1 pound cooked tuna steak, bone and skin removed, or
   tuna canned in water
¼ pound sweet butter, softened, cut into 8 pieces
2 tablespoons chopped fresh dill
1 teaspoon dry mustard
Salt and freshly ground white pepper to taste

Cut tuna into large chunks and place in a food processor. If using canned tuna, drain fish before placing in processor.

Process tuna while adding butter, one piece at a time. After half the butter has been added, add dill and mustard and continue processing until all ingredients are well combined. Season to taste and spoon rillettes into a 3-cup crock.

Cover rillettes and chill for 4 to 6 hours before serving.

Serves 6 to 8.

PÂTÉ D'ANCHOIS

On the northern fishing coast of France a popular pâté served in many local bistros is Pâté de Hareng Fumés—pâté of smoked herring. Smoked herrings are not always readily available in the United States, but anchovies, which are small herrings, can be easily found in cans and jars. Use fillets of anchovies in olive oil, do not use anchovy paste.

> **3–4 cans or jars of fillets of anchovies in olive oil (approximately 8 ounces)**
> **½ pound sweet butter, softened**
> **1 tablespoon lemon juice**
> **Pinch cayenne pepper**

Empty jars or cans of fillets of anchovies with oil into a food processor. Add butter, lemon juice, and cayenne and process until well combined.

Spoon pâté into two 1-cup crocks or into a 2-cup terrine. Cover and refrigerate for 4 hours.

Serves 6 to 8.

CHAPTER NINE

SAUCES AND OTHER GOOD THINGS

A successful offering of pâté depends upon the breads, sauces, and condiments that are served with it. After you've prepared a rich terrine of salmon it would be most unfortunate to present it with a store-bought sauce tartar, and it would certainly detract from a pâté de campagne to serve it with ordinary catsup. Homemade sauces will add an extra fillip to your pâtés, as will interesting breads, relishes, pickles, and condiments.

Breads

While French and Italian breads are natural accompaniments to pâtés, there's no reason to limit yourself to just these breads. Heavy black breads, pumpernickel and rye breads, as well as the dense corn-rye, are also excellent with coarse pâtés.

A smooth liver pâté deserves thinly sliced rye or pumpernickel, buttered, if you wish; and rillettes of pork is especially fine with whole-wheat bread, either Italian or French. Never diminish the value of an important pâté with a soft white bread, and crocks of pâtés such as eggplant or chicken rillettes deserve more than tiny crackers. Crackers are not the best match for most pâtés, but if crackers are a party favorite make sure they're generous in size.

The Mustard Story

Ball-park mustard tastes wonderful on a ball-park frank, and deli mustard is perfect on corned-beef-on-rye, but pâtés deserve other kinds of mustard. Dijon mustards, made with wine and spices, are right for pâtés. Today there are Dijon-type mustards made in the United States, and their sharper flavor makes them preferable to other American mustards.

In addition to Dijon mustards there are imported mustards made with a variety of herbs and spices, and most are good with pâtés, but some could overwhelm a pâté. A mustard heavily laced with garlic would definitely be too strong for a mild liver pâté, while it would be fine dabbed on chunks of a gâteau de viande.

A mustard worth investigating is moutarde à l'ancien, or a mustard prepared with the hulls of the mustard seed still in it. Remember this mustard when you're planning to take a pâté on a picnic.

Pickles and Such

In France a pâté is often accompanied by a large crock of tiny, whole cornichon pickles, which are served with wooden tongs. You can buy imported cornichons to serve with your pâtés, but if you don't want to pay the price for imported pickles, serve American tiny gherkins instead.

Other items that are delicious with many pâtés are Italian fruits in mustard, Indian mango chutney, American watermelon pickle, tiny black olives prepared Niçoise fashion, and wrinkle-skin Greek olives. Preparing your own Niçoise olives is simple, and far cheaper than the same olives bought in a fancy-food store. Consider, too, a batch of mixed pickles—carrots, peppers, and cauliflower—when you're serving slices of cold pâté, or present a bowl of crudités—carrot curls, tiny red radishes, cauliflower and broccoli flowerets, and cherry tomatoes—with any of the fish, vegetable or chicken pâtés served in a crock.

CASHEW CREAM SAUCE

2 cups chicken broth
1 cup dry white wine
1 tablespoon butter
1 tablespoon all-purpose flour
1 cup lightly toasted raw cashew nuts, coarsely chopped
1 cup heavy sweet cream (whipping cream)
Salt and freshly ground white pepper to taste

Combine chicken broth and wine in a saucepan and boil until reduced to 1 cup.

Melt butter in a skillet and add flour, whisking over medium heat for 1 minute. Add reduced broth and wine and bring to a boil while whisking. Add cashews.

Remove from heat and place in a food processor. Process until nuts are completely incorporated and sauce is smooth.

Return to saucepan and whisk in cream. Return to medium heat, whisking until sauce comes to a boil again. Add salt and pepper to taste.

Yield: 2½ cups, approximately

LEMON-CHIVE SABAYON

8 egg yolks
½ cup dry white Burgundy
3 tablespoons lemon juice
2 tablespoons chopped fresh chives
Salt and freshly ground white pepper to taste

Whisk egg yolks well in top of a double boiler and add wine and lemon juice. Cook, whisking constantly, over hot but not boiling water until sauce has thickened. It will take from 3 to 5 minutes, or until sauce coats a spoon thickly.

Remove from stove and set in a bowl of ice and water. Continue whisking until sauce is lukewarm. If sauce is too thick, beat in additional wine. Add chives and salt and pepper to taste.

Yield: 2½ cups, approximately

BEURRE BLANC SAUCE I

6 shallots, minced
2 cups dry white wine
12 tablespoons butter, cut into 12 pieces
Salt and freshly ground white pepper to taste

Combine shallots and wine in a saucepan and bring to a boil. Cook shallot-wine combination until reduced to about ½ cup.

Add butter 1 piece at a time while whisking sauce until all ingredients are thoroughly combined. Season to taste.

Yield: 1½ cups, approximately

BEURRE BLANC SAUCE II

¼ cup white vinegar
¼ cup dry white wine
1 tablespoon minced shallots or green onions (scallions)
Salt and freshly ground white pepper to taste
¼ pound plus 4 tablespoons butter
1 tablespoon lemon juice

Cook vinegar, wine, shallots or green onions, and seasonings in a saucepan until reduced by half. Cut butter into 12 pieces. Over very low heat, beat in butter, one piece at a time. Sauce will thicken. Remove from heat after all the butter has been incorporated and beat in lemon juice.

Serve at once, or keep warm in top of a double boiler over warm, not hot, water.

Yield: 1½ cups approximately

TOMATO SAUCE PROVENÇAL

2 tablespoons olive oil
2 garlic cloves, pressed
3 cups canned imported plum tomatoes
¼ teaspoon Herbes de Provence

Heat olive oil in a saucepan and sauté garlic cloves for 3 minutes, stirring. Add tomatoes and Herbes de Provence to saucepan and cook for 10 to 15 minutes, or until sauce thickens and liquid is reduced.

Yield: 2½ cups, approximately

ORANGE-LEMON SAUCE

2 tablespoons butter
1 teaspoon cornstarch
½ cup orange juice
¼ cup Dubonnet Blanc
2 tablespoons lemon juice

Heat butter in a small saucepan.

Combine cornstarch and orange juice, mixing thoroughly. Add orange juice mixture, Dubonnet Blanc, and lemon juice to butter. Cook, stirring, until sauce bubbles and thickens slightly.

Yield: 1 cup, approximately

SAUCE VERTE

2 cups mayonnaise
1 tablespoon lemon juice
1 tablespoon rinsed and coarsely chopped fillets of an-
**   chovies (optional)**
1 chopped green onion (scallion)
6 fresh basil leaves
1 cup tender spinach or sorrel leaves
Salt and freshly ground white pepper to taste

Place all ingredients in food processor and process until sauce is smooth and well blended. Refrigerate for 1 hour before using.

Yield: 2½ cups, approximately

PIMIENTO SAUCE

4 tablespoons butter
1 shallot, minced
1 cup dry white wine
½ cup heavy sweet cream (whipping cream)
1½ teaspoons Dijon mustard
¼ cup pureed pimiento peppers
8 tablespoons softened butter

Melt 4 tablespoons butter in a small saucepan; add shallot and sauté. Stir in wine and simmer until liquid is reduced by half.

Add cream and cook for 2 minutes, stirring occasionally. Stir in mustard and pureed pimiento. Beat in 8 tablespoons softened butter, a tablespoon at a time. Let sauce cool slightly before serving.

Yield: 1 cup, approximately

TOMATO CONCASSE

A tomato concasse is a sauce of crushed tomatoes, lightly sea-soned, with pieces of tomato still visible. It's not meant to be a smooth sauce or puree, and it can be prepared with either fresh or canned tomatoes.

> **12 plum tomatoes, *or* a 20-ounce can of Italian plum to-matoes, drained**
> **2 tablespoons butter**
> **¼ teaspoon thyme**
> **Salt and freshly ground black pepper to taste**

Chop tomatoes coarsely in a food processor and combine with butter in a saucepan. Cook over low heat, stirring, for 10 min-utes. Add seasonings and continue cooking until most of the liquid has evaporated.

Yield: 1½ cups approximately

WATERCRESS SAUCE

3 bunches watercress
2 cups crème fraîche (page 210)
Salt and freshly ground white pepper

Wash watercress thoroughly. Blanch watercress in boiling water for 1 minute. Drain, refresh with cold water, and drain again.

Chop watercress coarsely in a food processor. Place chopped watercress in a saucepan and cook, stirring, for approximately 3 minutes or until water evaporates.

Over low heat, gradually add crème fraîche to watercress, stirring. Add seasonings. Using a whisk, beat sauce until all ingredients are thoroughly combined. Serve sauce warm.

Yield: 3 cups, approximately

SAUCE CIBOULETTE

2 cups crème fraîche (page 210)
¼ teaspoon salt (optional)
¼ teaspoon white pepper
½ cup finely chopped chives

Combine all ingredients in a bowl and, using a whisk or hand beater, beat until thoroughly mixed and well combined.

Yield: 2 cups, approximately

MAYONNAISE I

2 egg yolks
¼ teaspoon salt
2 teaspoons Dijon mustard
3 teaspoons lemon juice
1 cup olive oil

Place all ingredients, except oil, in a food processor. Process briefly to combine.

With machine on, gradually add oil to other ingredients. Continue processing until mixture thickens—about 2 minutes.

Yield: 1½ cups, approximately

MAYONNAISE II

3 egg yolks
1 tablespoon lemon juice
¼ teaspoon salt
¼ teaspoon Dijon mustard
Pinch cayenne pepper
1 cup olive oil
1 cup vegetable oil

Place egg yolks, lemon juice, salt, mustard, and cayenne pepper in a processor. Process briefly to combine.

With machine on, gradually add oils to egg-yolk mixture. Continue processing until mayonnaise thickens.

Yield: 3 cups, approximately

PEPPERY ROUILLE SAUCE

This hot sauce, traditionally served with bouillabaisse, is also wonderful served with a fish pâté.

> 1 small, hot red chili pepper, seeded (use ½ pepper if you prefer sauce less hot)
> 1 medium potato, cooked
> 3 cloves garlic
> ½ tablespoon tomato paste, *or* 1 tablespoon tomato puree
> ½ cup olive oil
> Salt and freshly ground black pepper to taste

Place all ingredients, except for oil and salt and pepper, in food processor and puree.

Gradually add oil until sauce is thick and all ingredients are thoroughly combined. Season to taste.

Yield: 1 cup, approximately

AÏOLI

A garlic mayonnaise that's excellent with pâtés de campagne and other coarse-textured pâtés.

1 egg
2 teaspoons Dijon mustard
1 tablespoon wine vinegar
¼ teaspoon salt
¼ teaspoon freshly ground white pepper
3 cloves garlic
1 cup olive oil

Combine egg, mustard, vinegar, salt and pepper in food processor. Start processing and drop garlic into processor through feed tube.

Gradually add oil and process until mixture thickens—about 1 minute.

Yield: 1 cup, approximately

SHRIMP SAUCE

1 tablespoon butter
1 tablespoon all-purpose flour
1 cup light sweet cream
**¼ pound large shrimp, shelled, deveined, and coarsely
    chopped**
2 tablespoons dry sherry
Salt and freshly ground white pepper to taste

Heat butter in top of a double boiler. Stir in flour and gradually add cream, stirring. Add shrimp, sherry, and seasonings
and cook for 3 to 5 minutes, or until sauce is hot and shrimp
are cooked.

Yield: 2½ cups, approximately

TOMATO SHISO
VINAIGRETTE SAUCE

12 plum tomatoes, *or* **a 20-ounce can of Italian plum tomatoes, drained**
¼ teaspoon thyme
Salt and freshly ground black pepper to taste
**10 leaves shiso (Japanese beefsteak plant), cut into ju-
lienne strips**
1 tablespoon sherry vinegar
4 tablespoons olive oil

Chop tomatoes coarsely and combine with thyme, salt and
pepper in a saucepan. Cook, over low heat, stirring, until most
of the liquid has evaporated and you have a coarse puree.
Allow puree to cool for 20 minutes.

Combine shiso leaves, sherry vinegar, and olive oil in a small
bowl. Mix thoroughly and pour over tomato mixture. Allow
sauce to blend for 1 hour before serving.

Yield: 1½ cups, approximately

CHIVE MUSTARD SAUCE

½ cup Dijon mustard
½ cup olive oil
¼ cup coarsely chopped chives
Salt and freshly ground black pepper to taste

Combine all ingredients in a food processor and process until mixture is thoroughly blended.

Yield: 1 cup, approximately

BEURRE ÀL'ÉCHALOTE SAUCE

1 teaspoon finely chopped shallots
1 tablespoon dry white wine
⅓ cup heavy sweet cream (whipping cream)
Pinch of saffron
¼ pound butter, cut into 1-inch dice
Salt and freshly ground white pepper to taste

Combine shallots and white wine in a small saucepan and reduce over low heat until liquid has completely evaporated.

Stir in cream and add saffron. Cook, stirring, over low heat until mixture is reduced by half.

Add all the butter at one time and continue cooking, stirring, until butter is completely absorbed by cream. Season to taste and keep warm in top of double boiler until ready to serve.

Yield: 1 cup, approximately

LOBSTER SAUCE

1 tablespoon finely chopped shallots
1 tablespoon cognac
Pinch of chopped fresh or dried tarragon
⅓ cup heavy sweet cream (whipping cream)
⅔ cup lobster bisque (homemade or canned)
Salt and freshly ground white pepper to taste

Combine shallots, cognac, and tarragon in a saucepan. Heat and cook until liquid is reduced by half. Add cream and cook, stirring, until mixture is again reduced by half.

Stir in lobster bisque and cook over low heat for 5 minutes. Season to taste and keep warm in top of double boiler until ready to serve.

Yield: 1 cup, approximately

HOLLANDAISE SAUCE

3 egg yolks
2 tablespoons lemon juice
¼ teaspoon salt (optional)
⅛ teaspoon freshly ground white pepper
¼ pound butter, melted

Combine egg yolks, lemon juice, and seasonings in a food processor and blend for a few seconds until combined.

Gradually add melted butter and continue processing until sauce thickens.

Yield: 1 cup, approximately

CAVIAR SAUCE

½ cup heavy sweet cream (whipping cream)
½ cup sour cream
2 tablespoons minced chives
4 ounces Golden Caviar or salmon caviar

Combine sweet cream, sour cream, and chives in a bowl. Stir to combine thoroughly.

Fold in caviar gently.

Yield: 1½ cups, approximately

HORSERADISH CREAM SAUCE

One 3-inch piece of fresh horseradish root, *or* 4 table-
    spoons bottled, grated horseradish
1 cup heavy sweet cream, lightly whipped
Sugar to taste
Salt and freshly ground white pepper to taste

Using a food processor, grate horseradish. Combine with all other ingredients and blend thoroughly.

Yield: 1½ cups, approximately

COLD PEANUT SAUCE
FROM THE BALI ROOM

1 cup peanut butter
2 ounces fresh lime juice
½ teaspoon sesame oil
2 pinches Chinese Five-Spice Powder
¼ teaspoon wine vinegar
1 pinch salt
4 ounces cold water
2 hard-cooked eggs, finely chopped

Combine all ingredients in a food processor and process until thoroughly blended.

Yield: 1½ cups, approximately

DILL SAUCE

1 cup mayonnaise
1 cup sour cream
4 tablespoons chopped fresh dill
⅛ teaspoon cumin
Salt and freshly ground white pepper to taste

Combine all ingredients in a bowl and mix, blending thoroughly. Refrigerate for 30 minutes before using.

Yield: 2 cups, approximately

BÉCHAMEL SAUCE

2 tablespoons butter
2 tablespoons all-purpose flour
½ cup light sweet cream
½ cup chicken broth
Salt and freshly ground white pepper to taste

Heat the butter in a saucepan and stir in flour. Cook, stirring, over low heat for 2 to 3 minutes, or until flour has lost its raw look. Be careful not to allow flour to brown.

Combine cream and broth and add gradually to flour-butter mixture. Cook, stirring, over very low heat until mixture is smooth and thick. Season to taste and keep warm over a Flame Tamer or in top of a double boiler until ready to use.

If sauce thickens too much before you wish to use it, stir in additional cream or chicken broth.

Yield: 1 cup, approximately

SAUCE DIJON

An excellent sauce to complement a petit pain de viande, or a gâteau de viande.

1 cup beef broth
½ cup dry red wine
2 shallots, minced
¼ teaspoon Herbes de Provence
1 tablespoon Dijon mustard
3 tablespoons butter, softened, cut into bits

Combine all ingredients, except for butter, in a saucepan. Bring to a simmer and cook for 5 minutes, or until sauce reduces and is slightly thickened. Gradually add butter, stirring until it is blended into the sauce. Serve hot.

Yield: 1 cup, approximately

PLUM SAUCE

This sweetly tart sauce is especially delicious with game pâtés and terrines and is a nice accompaniment for the heavier gâteaux de viandes and veal tourtes.

2 pounds purple plums (Italian plums)
¼–½ cup sugar
1 cup orange juice
1 teaspoon lemon juice
2 tablespoons brandy
One 3-inch strip lemon peel

Remove pits from plums and combine plums with all other ingredients in a heavy saucepan. Cover, and cook over low heat for 30 to 40 minutes, or until plum halves have fallen apart and all ingredients are combined in a thick sauce. Correct seasoning.

Serves 6 to 8.

SAUCE CHAMPIGNON

4 tablespoons butter
1 small onion, chopped
¼ pound mushroom caps, thinly sliced
¼ cup dry white wine
1 cup crème fraîche (page 210) or sour cream
Salt and freshly ground white pepper to taste

Heat butter in a skillet and sauté onion, stirring, for 2 minutes. Add sliced mushrooms and continue sautéing until mushroom liquid is released. Add wine and cook until liquid is reduced by half.

Over low heat, stir in crème fraîche or sour cream and heat, stirring, until all ingredients are combined and sauce is hot. Season and spoon into a sauce bowl.

Yield: 1½ cups, approximately

SHRIMP BUTTER

¼ pound butter, softened
8 medium shrimp, cooked, and finely chopped
¼ teaspoon freshly ground white pepper
1 tablespoon finely chopped fresh dillweed

Place all ingredients in a food processor and process until just combined. Spoon Shrimp Butter into a small crock or individual soufflé dish and refrigerate for 1–2 hours before using.

Yield: 1 cup, approximately

MUSTARD BUTTER

Going on a picnic? Take along a pâté de campagne, a long loaf of French bread, and a crock of Mustard Butter.

4 tablespoons butter, softened
2 teaspoons Dijon mustard

Combine ingredients in a food processor and process until blended.

Yield: ½ cup, approximately

CLEAR ASPIC I

3 cups chicken or beef broth, or stock
2 tablespoons plain gelatin (2 packets)
1 teaspoon lemon juice
1 tablespoon dry sherry wine

Heat broth or stock. Stir in gelatin. Add lemon juice and sherry and continue stirring until gelatin is dissolved. Allow to cool.

Aspic can be used to glaze pâtés or, once it's set, aspic may be chopped and used as a garnish around base of a pâté.

Yield: 3 cups, approximately

CLEAR ASPIC II

    3 cups chicken or beef stock
    2 tablespoons plain gelatin (2 packets)
    1 egg white, lightly beaten
    1 eggshell, crushed
    2 tablespoons brandy or dry sherry wine

Pour stock into a saucepan and add gelatin, egg white, and crushed eggshell. (The egg white and eggshell are used to clarify the stock.)

Bring mixture to a boil, stirring constantly. Remove from heat and allow to stand for 5 minutes. Strain through a sieve lined with cheesecloth. Stir in brandy or sherry.

Yield: 3 cups, approximately

CLEAR ASPIC III

    1 can (10½ ounces) condensed beef bouillon
    2 tablespoons sherry or Madeira wine
    1 tablespoon (1 packet) unflavored gelatin, softened in 2
        tablespoons cold water

Heat all ingredients together, stirring until gelatin is dissolved.

Yield: 1 cup, approximately

CHAUD-FROID SAUCE

3 tablespoons butter
¼ cup all-purpose flour
4 cups chicken broth
2 tablespoons unflavored gelatin (2 packets)
½ cup dry sherry wine or cold water
½ cup heavy sweet cream (whipping cream)

Heat butter in a large saucepan. Stir in flour and remove from heat.

Heat chicken broth and add to butter-flour mixture, stirring or whisking. Bring to a simmer and cook for 5 to 10 minutes, or until mixture thickens.

Soften gelatin in sherry or water and add to sauce. Stir until gelatin is dissolved. Gradually add cream to sauce, mixing to combine. Allow chaud-froid to cool but not to set.

When using chaud-froid, set container in a bowl of hot water or chaud-froid may become too firm before entire glazing process is completed.

Yield: 5 cups, approximately

BASIL TOMATO RELISH

This spicy relish makes a fine and colorful accompaniment to a cold pâté.

> ½ cup (packed) fresh basil leaves
> 2 large, ripe tomatoes, peeled and quartered
> ¼–½ teaspoon hot red pepper flakes, or to taste
> Salt to taste
> 1 tablespoon olive oil

Place all ingredients in a food processor and process just until tomatoes are coarsely chopped and all ingredients are thoroughly combined.

Yield: 1½ cups, approximately

SICILIAN OLIVE RELISH

Serve with the Italian Torta of Spinach and Ricotta Cheese, the Roman Torta, or any of the coarse-textured pâtés or pork rillettes.

> **2 cups drained, tiny black olives (California ripe olives) with pits**
> **½ cup olive oil**
> **1 clove garlic**
> **¼ teaspoon Herbes de Provence**
> **1 teaspoon red wine vinegar or Balsamic vinegar**
> **1½-inch piece orange rind**
> **⅛ teaspoon hot red pepper flakes**

Place olives in a bowl. Reserve.

Blend all ingredients, except for olives, in a food processor, until thoroughly mixed. Pour sauce over olives.

Refrigerate for 3–4 hours before serving and stir every hour.

Yield: 2 cups, approximately

OLIVES NIÇOISE

**1 cup drained, tiny black olives (California ripe olives),
 with pits**
½ cup olive oil
1 teaspoon Herbes de Provence, finely crushed
1 clove garlic, pressed

Combine all ingredients in a bowl and mix thoroughly. Refrigerate overnight before serving.

Yield: 1 cup, approximately

CRÈME FRAÎCHE

1 cup sour cream
2 cups heavy sweet cream (whipping cream)

Combine sour cream and sweet cream in a heavy saucepan. Mix thoroughly.

Heat cream mixture over low heat, stirring continuously. Do not allow mixture to come to a simmer. When mixture is warm, pour into a container and cover partially. Allow cream mixture to remain unrefrigerated for 8 hours, or overnight, by which time cream will be thick. Stir and refrigerate until needed.

Yield: 3 cups

BASIC QUATRE-ÉPICES

A combination of four spices—pepper, cloves, cinnamon or ginger, and nutmeg—can be readily bought in French food stores. You can, however, make your own quatre-épices, and this spice mixture can be used for pâtés, stews, roast and grilled meats. As you become more familiar with the flavor of the quatre-épices you have made, you can modify it to your own taste, perhaps substituting basil for ginger, thyme for cloves, and creating a spicy combination that will be your own unique blend.

> **4 tablespoons whole white peppercorns**
> **½ tablespoon whole cloves**
> **½ tablespoon ground cinnamon or ginger**
> **½ tablespoon ground nutmeg**

Combine all ingredients and grind in a spice mill, blender, or coffee mill until finely ground and well combined.

Spoon into a screw-top jar and seal tightly.

Yield: ½ cup, approximately

CRÊPES WITH DILL

1 cup all-purpose flour
¼ teaspoon salt
3 eggs
4 tablespoons melted butter
1½ cups milk
4 tablespoons minced fresh dill
Butter for cooking crêpes

Using a food processor, combine all ingredients, except dill and butter, and process until mixture is thoroughly combined, and has the consistency of heavy cream. Stir in dill. Allow crêpe mixture to rest in refrigerator for 1 hour.

Butter a 6-inch crêpe pan. Using a small ladle or a 2-tablespoon measuring cup, pour enough batter into pan to coat the bottom. Tilt the pan and cook crêpe over medium high heat until lightly browned. Turn crêpe and cook on other side. Slide crêpe out of pan onto a large, flat platter. Continue cooking until batter is used up, separating layers of crêpes with sheets of waxed paper.

Yield: 16–20 crêpes

NASI PUTIH
(Indonesian Steamed Rice)

6 ounces long-grain rice
8 ounces fresh or frozen coconut milk
1 pinch ground salam (Indonesian bay leaf)
1 pinch salt

Wash and rinse rice three times. Drain, and cover rice with cold water, allowing rice to remain in water for 30 minutes.

In a saucepan, combine coconut milk, bay leaf, and salt and mix thoroughly. Add rice and cook over low heat until rice is tender and liquid is absorbed.

If rice is not tender after coconut milk has been absorbed, add hot water, 2 tablespoons at a time, until rice is cooked.

Serves 4 to 6.

CHAPTER TEN

CLEVER COMBINATIONS

There are some pâtés that seem so suitable for every meal, every party, every occasion, that there is a temptation to serve them again and again. However, with the variety available, each dinner, buffet, or special lunch can present a new offering of pâté. Pâtés combine well with other courses, as the suggested menus indicate. Suggested is the key word, and creative chefs and party-givers will want to develop combinations to suit their own personal bias and tastes.

Sunday Brunch

Mimosas—orange juice and champagne
Orange framboisée—orange juice with a splash of real raspberry syrup
Terrine of Salmon from the Loire Valley
Sauce Ciboulette
Buttered rounds of French bread
Salad of endive and watercress with oil and vinegar dressing
Curried Chicken Liver Pâté
Party rye bread slices, buttered
Camembert cheese

Grapes
Coffee
Italian almond biscuits

Sunday Supper

Bloody Marys
Spiced tomato juice with lime wedges
White wine spritzers
Sparkling water with fresh lime juice
Brandied Pâté
Thinly sliced black bread
Italian Torta of Spinach and Ricotta Cheese
Orange and grapefruit salad
Vanilla ice cream with hot chocolate sauce
Espresso

The Little Dinner

Campari and soda
Red wine kir—red wine with a splash of cassis
Dry sherry
Rillettes of Chicken from Bresse
Pumpernickel bread slices
Tourte of Pork with Onions from Alsace
Romaine and escarole salad with oil and vinegar dressing
Cold lemon mousse *or*
Lemon sorbet
Coffee or Espresso

The Important Buffet Dinner Party

Kir royale—champagne with a splash of cassis or framboise li-
    queur
Club soda and bitters
Egg and Vegetable Terrine
Caviar Sauce

Terrine of Fresh Duck Liver Pâté with Pistachios from Four-
nou's Ovens
Pâté of Smoked Fish
Lemon-Chive Sabayon Sauce
Salad of Bibb or Boston lettuce with oil and vinegar dressing
Tiny éclairs, cream puffs, and lemon cookies
Coffee or espresso
Brandy and liqueurs
Sugared grape clusters

The Five-to-Seven Apéritif Party

Kriter or other sparkling white wine
White wine kir—white wine with a splash of cassis
Dubonnet Blanc
Lillet
Mineral water with lime wedges
Tangerine juice on the rocks
Assortment of Rillettes:
    Rillettes de Porc
    Rillettes de Saumon
    Rillettes of Eggs Maharajah
Pâté Pantin with Aspic
Chicken Spinach Terrine
Baskets of assorted breads and French rolls, sliced
Miniature croissants

The Instead-of-a-Barbecue Party

Iced tea
Iced coffee
Sangría
Tapenade
Gâteau Américain en Croûte
Sliced tomato and onion salad with fresh basil and oil and vin-
egar dressing
Fresh melon slices, with or without ice cream
Chocolate cookies

New Year's Day Dinner

Hot mulled wine
Cold cider
Rillettes de Aubergine
Dry red Burgundy
New Year's Day Pork Pie
Puree of spinach
Puree of carrots
Pineapple chunks with crème Chantilly
Coffee

Index